NVQ/SVQ workbook. level 2

PREPARATION & COOKING

To be used in conjunction with the following:

Practical Cookery **(eighth edition)**
The Theory of Catering **(eighth edition)**
Candidates Achievement Logbook

Aims: to develop the knowledge of students taking NVQ level 2 in Food Preparation and Cooking

Hodder & Stoughton

A MEMBER OF THE HODDER HEADLINE GROUP

Victor Ceserani MBE, CPA, MBA, FHCIMA
Formerly Head of The Ealing School of Hotelkeeping and Catering (now Thames Valley University)
and
Professor David Foskett BEd (Hons), FHCIMA
Head of Programmes, Thames Valley University, London

British Library Cataloguing in Publication Data

Ceserani, Victor
  NVQ/SVQ Workbook. – Level 2: Food
  Preparation and Cooking
  I. Title   II. Foskett, David
  641.5

  ISBN 0 340 630760

First published 1995
Impression number 10 9 8 7 6 5 4 3 2 1
Year   1998 1997 1996 1995

Typeset by Wearset, Boldon, Tyne and Wear.
Printed in Great Britain for Hodder & Stoughton Educational, a division of Hodder Headline Plc, 338 Euston Road, London NW1 3BH by The Bath Press, Avon

Contents

Introduction

In addition to learning the skills of food preparation and cooking, it is also necessary to be aware of the health, safety and hygiene factors that must at all times be practised to comply with Government legislation. Furthermore, as more and more people are conscious of healthy eating so the need for knowledge of simple nutrition principles is required.

Readers are advised to develop an attitude of mind so that whenever they are working in practical situations, they not only think about why various processes are used but also understand fully the reasons why certain commodities are chosen for specific purposes.

When working through this book think of practical work in relation to the theory. This not only complements the theory but also helps to develop a deeper understanding.

Readers possessing a *Candidates Achievement Logbook* will find that it will contain many of the suggested responses to questions asked in this workbook.

Unit NG1

Maintain a safe and secure working environment

NG1.1 *Maintain personal health and hygiene*

Read pages 16–17 of *Practical Cookery*.

1 What general hygiene practices must be followed in your work environment?

   ....

   ....

2 Why must correct clothing, footwear and headgear be worn at all times?

   ....

3 Why are chefs' jackets double-breasted and aprons worn below the knees?

   ....

4 Why is it unwise to wear sandals or training shoes in the kitchen?

   ....

5 Why should staff involved in food preparation and cooking wear a head covering?

   ....

6 All clothing should be clean, in good repair and (where appropriate) pressed.

7 Body perspiration and underarm odours can quickly occur, particularly in busy
   situations and warm rooms. Any suspicion of this is most objectionable to customers,
   guests and fellow members of staff.
   • Excluding the use of body sprays and underarm deodorants, what are the two ways
     in which perspiration or odour can be avoided?

   ....

   ....

8   Trousers, shirts, dresses, jackets and overalls should be kept on proper hangers.
   • Why is this necessary?

   ....

9   Many staff spend a large part of their working time on their feet, so practical,
   comfortable shoes are essential.
   • Calculate the number of hours that you spend on your feet during a working day.

   ....

Shoes should be kept clean and in good repair; if lace-ups are worn the laces should
always be tied. A second pair of shoes kept at work can help relieve aching feet during a
long working day.

10   Correct clothing, footwear and headgear should be worn at all times when on duty in
   order to:
   a   prevent accidents, e.g. safe shoes in the kitchen protect feet from damage from
       hot spillage of fat, oil, etc.
   b   prevent cross-contamination and infection, e.g. dirty clothes enable germs to
       multiply, and if dirty clothing comes into contact with food the food may be
       contaminated;
   c   maintain a clean and professional appearance, e.g. neat, clean and helpful food
       service staff add to the enjoyment of a meal for a customer;
   d   support the company image, e.g. guests that are impressed with the appearance of
       the staff inevitably form good opinions about the company and are likely to return
       – without customers you have no job!;
   e   ensure the safety of the person, e.g. a loose heel on a shoe may come off when you
       are hurrying downstairs, which may result in you injuring yourself;
   f   comply with the law, e.g. if hair is found in prepared food, the worker is liable to
       prosecution and a fine.
   • Give three examples of incorrect working clothing that you have seen worn.

   ....

   ....

   ....

11   Why should food handler's hair be washed regularly and kept covered?

   ....

12   Why is it advisable to keep hair neat, and under control?

   ....

13 Why should hair never be scratched or combed by food handlers?

....

14 Jewellery, perfumes and cosmetics should only be worn in accordance with procedures laid down by your employer.

15 What is the risk from a food handler wearing jewellery, e.g. clip-on earrings?

....

If make-up is used, it should only be used sparingly. If perfumes or aftershave are used by staff working in food preparation areas, they may taint the food.

16 Cuts, grazes, burns, wounds must be correctly treated.
   • Should they be kept covered? ....
   • If yes, with what should they be covered, and why?

....

17 Why and to whom should illness and infections be reported?

....

18 With certain spots, cuts, and sores there are vast numbers of harmful bacteria which must not be permitted to get on food.
   • Should people who have septic spots, cuts, and sores be allowed to handle food? If not, why not?

....

   • What is meant by the word septic?

....

19 Hygiene instruction should form part of an induction programme for staff, and should be a continuing process throughout employment.
   Why?

....

....

....

20 Why is it important to maintain good personal hygiene?

....

....

21 All food handlers, with the exception of waiters, waitresses and persons serving only drinks, are required by law to wear clean and washable overclothing. Why is this?

....

....

22 Why is it essential to use correct lifting techniques?

....

23 Why is it important to comply with health and safety legislation?

....

24 Where and from whom can current information on health and safety be obtained?

....

<u>NG1.2</u> *Carry out procedures in the event of a fire*

Read pages 2–4 of *Practical Cookery*.

1 List the possible causes of fire in the working environment.

....

....

....

....

• What preventative actions can be taken in each case to minimise the risk of fire?

....

....

....

....

2 If in doubt about the scale or size of a fire, break the glass on the nearest fire alarm system and telephone the fire brigade.
  - What number would you dial for the fire brigade?

....

3 What establishment procedures should be followed in the event of a fire?

....

....

4 Do not panic but warn other people nearby.
  - How would you warn other people?

....

5 List the fire alarms in your establishment and how they are activated.

....

....

....

....

6 Read the fire instructions of your establishment and always follow them.

7 Close all doors and windows and turn off the gas, electricity and ventilating fans.
  - What could happen if you fail to close doors and windows?

....

8 Why should a fire never be approached unless it is safe to do so?

....

....

9 Do not wait for the fire to get out of control before calling the fire brigade.

10 Do not risk your own safety or that of others.

11 If the fire is a small one, use the appropriate fire extinguisher.
- What is the correct extinguisher to use on a fat fire?

....

- What is the correct extinguisher to use on a wood, paper, etc., fire?

....

- What is the correct extinguisher to use on fires involving gas?

....

12 Fire fighting equipment must only be used in accordance with laid-down procedures.
- Why is a carbon dioxide (CO_2) gas extinguisher not the most efficient way of putting out a fat fire?

....

- What is the colour of the container of a CO_2 extinguisher?

....

13 Safety and emergency signs and notices must be strictly adhered to.
- What is the purpose of a fire-blanket?

....

14 Leave the building by the nearest fire escape route and be prepared to assist anyone who may be in need of help. Make for the laid-down assembly point and wait for the roll-call.
- What is the purpose of a roll-call?

....

15 Failure to carry out one or any of the other points may lead to severe damage of property, injury, severe burns and loss of life.

16 Established procedures.
It is the responsibility of your employer to see that all relevant procedures in case of

fire are made readily available to you. It is your responsibility to ensure that you have read and fully understood what action is required of you in case of fire.

17 A fire alarm is a means of warning people. It should be capable of being operated without exposing anyone to any undue risk.
   - The alarm should also be ....
   - The alarm signal should also be distinctive. Why?

   ....

   - Fire detectors are activated by:

   a Smoke

   b ....

   c ....

   - It is also possible to link these detectors into a central alarm point which instantly notifies the ....

   - Heat and smoke detectors must never be painted. Why?

   ....

   - Why and how, are cigarettes likely to start fires?

   ....

   - Power supply equipment used for emergency lighting must not be used for any other purpose. Why?

   ....

   - State the three principal methods to extinguishing a fire.

   ....

   ....

   ....

- Write down the procedures for evacuating the building in which you are working or studying, in the event of a fire.

....

....

....

....

18 Why is it important to comply with health and safety legislation?

....

....

19 Where and from whom can information on current health and safety be obtained?

....

NG1.3 *Maintain a safe environment for customers, staff and visitors*

Read pages 10–15 of *Practical Cookery*.

1 What preventative action can be taken to maintain a safe environment for customers, staff and visitors?

....

....

2 What are the potential hazards within your own working environment?

....

3 Why should suspicious items and packages not be approached or tampered with?

....

4 Any item or package which may give cause for suspicion must be left untouched, e.g. tins, boxes, parcels, carrier bags and holdalls which may seem strange to you and may

be left in a strange place, whether in full view, part hidden or hidden.
- If you find a strange sports holdall by, or on top of your locker, should it be treated with suspicion? Why?

....

5 If a suspicious package is found, report it immediately to your departmental head so that prompt action may be taken. The package may contain a bomb or fire explosives. Do not panic! In a calm voice, warn others nearby to keep away until the package has been dealt with.

6 Any bag, package or parcel which is left unattended by a stranger for no apparent reason must be treated as suspicious.
- What would you do if you found a carton of duty-free cigarettes left half hidden in a corner?

....

7 Resist the temptation to 'take a peep'. It might lead to injury or death to you and those near you.

8 It is your employer's responsibility to make you aware of the correct health and safety procedures to be followed if a suspicious package is found. It is your responsibility to fully understand and to know what action to take. If you are unsure, consult your trainer or tutor.
- Write down the instructions you have been given by your line manager or tutor if you discover a suspicious item or package.

....

....

....

....

9 Notice of accidents is important under the Social Security (claims and payments) Regulations 1979.
- These regulations further require the employer to give the relevant social security office which particulars?

....

....

....

- The 'appropriate particulars' are full name, address, occupation of injured persons and:

....

....

10 Major injury accidents are defined as:
- Give some examples

....

....

....

....

- Who is the enforcement authority responsible for your establishment?

....

....

11 Where is the first aid and accident register located in your establishment?

....

12 When an accident occurs the member of staff responsible for first aid must be called immediately.
- Name three common types of accidents.

....

....

....

13 If the accident is severe and if a person qualified in first aid is not on the scene, then an ambulance must be called.
- What number should be dialled to call an ambulance? ....
- What is the appropriate action to ensure the safety of injured and non-injured persons?

....

- Why is it important for you to be aware of the laid-down procedures in your establishment?

  ....

14 If you are waiting for a person qualified in first aid to arrive at the scene of the emergency, lie the injured person down and keep him or her warm by covering him or her with a blanket or clothing.
   - If an injured person shows signs of faintness, sickness, clammy skin and a pale face, what is the likely conditions or ailment they are suffering? ....

15 All accidents must be reported to the employer and a record of the accident entered in the Accident Book.
   - Familiarise yourself with the first-aid procedures in the event of: shock, fainting, cuts, nosebleeds, fractures, burns and scalds, electric shock, gassing.

16 Every employed earner who suffers personal injury by accident in respect of which benefit may be payable must give notice of such accident, either verbally or in writing, as soon as possible as practicable after the event, provided that any such notice may be given by some other person acting on his/her behalf.
   - Every such notice must be given to his/her ....
     or one of his/her ....
     or to any official under whose ....
     he/she is employed at the time of the accident or to any person designated for the purpose by the employer and must be given the appropriate particulars.

17 Who in your establishment is responsible for first aid?

  ....

18 What is your responsibility in relation to health and safety legislation?

  ....

19 Why is it important to comply with health and safety legislation?

  ....

20 Where and from whom can current information on health and safety legislation be obtained?

  ....

NG1.4 *Maintain a secure environment for customers, staff and visitors*

Read pages 11–15 of *Practical Cookery*.

1   Which keys, property and areas should be secured against unauthorised access at all times?

    ....

2   Why is it essential to be aware of potential security risks?

    ....

When customers and visitors are in a hotel, they have the right to demand that the premises and procedures used are safe, secure and hygienic. Customers may be staying in the establishment for a holiday or for a visit to a local business centre.

3   For security precaution reasons how should the following be dealt with:

    a Contractors and salesmen

    ....

    ....

    b Deliveries

    ....

    ....

4   Staff training is effective in making staff security conscious. This is regarded as an important weapon against crime. Summarise any training you have been given.

    ....

    ....

    ....

    ....

    ....

....

....

5 Who in your establishment or training environment is responsible for security?

....

6 Why should there be a regular review procedure for security?

....

....

7 If you have to bring a large sum of money to work, is it safer to keep it in your locker or on your person?

....

8 What particular items of food are vulnerable to theft and why? Give three examples.

....

....

....

9 Can you name any examples of theft connected with alcoholic beverages that you have been aware of?

....

....

10 Why should keys never be left in locks or in odd places such as desk drawers?

....

11 Name three other places where you have seen keys kept.

....

12 Why is it important to report all unusual or non-routine incidents to the appropriate person?

....

13 Why should only disclosable information be given to others?

....

14 What procedures relating to lost property must be adhered to?

....

15 Why is it important to comply with health and safety legislation?

....

16 Where and from whom can current information on health and safety legislation be obtained?

....

Record of Achievement – Completion of Unit NG1

Candidate's signature: _____

Assessor's signature: _____

Date: _____

Unit 2NG4

Create and maintain effective working relationships

2NG4.1 *Establish and maintain working relationships with other members of staff*

Read pages 17–22 of *Practical Cookery*.

1 What is your own work role, and what are your responsibilities?

....

2 Why is it important to understand methods of establishing constructive relationships? Give two examples from your own experience.

....

....

3 When is it necessary to seek and exchange information and obtain advice and support? Give an example.

....

4 What procedures need to be followed when handling disagreements and conflict?

....

....

5 Why is it essential to be discreet when handling confidential information?

....

6 Why is it necessary to inform and consult with others about problems and proposals?

....

7 Why is it necessary to communicate proposals for change?

....

8 Why may it be necessary to use appropriate actions and different styles of approach in different situations?

....

9 What are the employee's responsibilities in complying with equal opportunity legislation?

....

10 List the potential benefits of teamwork in the working situation.

....

....

....

• Suggest ways in which effective teamwork can be achieved.

....

....

11 When items of equipment are used by various people, what should be the golden rule followed by each worker when they have finished using the equipment? Support your answer with examples of bad habits that you have observed.

....

....

....

12 Give your views on criticism of your work performance by your supervisors and indicate the type of criticism that you react best to, giving two or three examples.

....

....

....

13 Write your views, with examples, on:

    a being positive

    ....

    ....

    b being assertive

    ....

    ....

14 Give your opinions, with examples in each case, on the following three methods of communication:

    a speaking

    ....

    ....

    b listening

    ....

    ....

    c body language

    ....

    ....

15 What are your views, with examples, on the importance of the following in communication?

    a facial expression

    ....

    ....

b gestures

....

....

c space

....

....

16 Think back over the education and training that you have received and select the person that you consider had the most effective way of communicating knowledge. List the various points that have made you make the choice.

....

....

....

17 Self development is important if one wishes to progress and improve performance. Set out your ideas on a self development programme.

....

....

....

....

18 Contributions to the development of others is something that should be considered when possible. List, with examples, ways in which this can be carried out:

a for colleagues

....

....

b for new members of staff

....

....

19 Think back to your own introduction into the industry. How could it have been improved?

....

....

20 If you were asked for advice from a school leaver on how to enter the catering industry and develop a sound career, what would your advice be?

....

....

21 Consider the time that you have spent in training so far. Write your ideas on how you would like your career to progress over the coming years.

....

....

....

2NG4.2 *Receive and assist visitors*

Working in the Hotel and Catering Industry is about working and coming into contact with people. It is important to remember that people visiting our hotel or restaurant often have a choice in where they dine or sleep. People therefore expect to be greeted by staff who are both courteous and polite. Treat visitors as guests.
The following should be remembered and practised:

a Be polite and helpful at all times.
b Identify the guests' needs, and deal with them promptly and accurately.
c Describe the products and services of the restaurant, hotel or organisation accurately and promptly as appropriate.

The establishment should adopt a clear policy on greeting visitors. The internal methods of communication must be clear, with the staff understanding exactly what is expected of them when dealing with customers. Both front of house and back of house must respond to the needs of customers. All staff need to know that they are employed to serve and support customers' needs and expectations. Any difficulties in understanding communication between staff and customers should be openly acknowledged, and appropriate help sought to alleviate the problems. This is also true if there are any difficulties emerging in providing support to guests. All guests' records should be kept up to date, legible and accurate.

Staff also need training to deal with difficult guests. The awkward customer of today must become the valued customer of tomorrow.

1   Why is it necessary to be positive when dealing with customers?

    ....

2   When speaking to customers, state why the volume and pitch of your voice has to be right.

    ....

3   What relationship is there, if any, between listening and facial expression?

    ....

4   Describe why receiving customers should be carried out in a professional manner.

    ....

    ....

5   What routine procedures apply to receiving and assisting visitors?

    ....

    ....

6   Who in your establishment is responsible for greeting and assisting visitors?

    ....

7   Outline your organisational procedures for greeting and assisting customers.

    ....

    ....

8   Do you consider these procedures to be right?

    ....

9   Do you feel that these procedures could be improved? If so, how?

....

10   State what you understand to be your role in relation to greeting and assisting customers.

....

11   How would you deal with a difficult customer in a restaurant?

....

12   How would you deal with a customer in a restaurant who had too much alcohol and became aggressive?

....

13   Establishments often have laid-down procedures for dealing with awkward and difficult customers. State your establishment's procedures.

....

....

14   Referring to your establishment, a college, what procedures must be followed when dealing with emergencies.

....

....

....

15   What services does your establishment provide to customers?

....

16   Who in your establishment has the main responsibility for greeting and assisting customers?

....

17   State how a chef working in the kitchen may assist customers in a restaurant or hotel.

....

18 What is the purpose of a paging system?

....

19 Describe the different ways in which services are communicated to customers.

....

....

20 Describe some of the legislation which aims to protect customers.

....

....

....

21 If you have any responsibility in your current employment for receiving and assisting visitors, state what you are required to do.

....

....

22 Visitors' requirements are very often predictable. As practising professional caterers, we are also required to deal with unexpected requests from our paying guests.
  • State any unexpected requests from customers you have had to deal with in your establishment.

....

....

23 Enquiries from guests can often be routine, but some can be complex.

  a Describe what you understand to be a routine enquiry.

....

  b Describe a complex enquiry.

....

24 Welcoming visitors and making them feel comfortable is an important aspect of the hospitality industry. Making them feel safe and secure is another.
- Briefly outline the security system which operates in your establishment.

....

....

25 Visiting other establishments to assess the way in which other organisations receive and assist customers is important.
- If you have recently visited an establishment as a customer, how were you received?

....

- Did you consider you were well treated? If not, how could the service be improved?

....

26 If you have difficulties in providing support to visitors, why should you openly acknowledge this and seek appropriate help?

....

....

27 Why is it important that records of any visits made are complete, legible and accurate?

....

28 What are the employee's responsibilities in complying with equal opportunities legislation?

....

Record of Achievement – Completion of Unit 2NG4

Candidate's signature: _____

Assessor's signature: _____

Date: _____

Unit 1ND1

Clean food production areas, equipment and utensils

1ND1.1 *Clean food production areas*

Read pages 37–39 of *Practical Cookery*.

1   Why is it important that work is planned and time appropriately allocated to meet daily schedules?

....

....

....

2   Sinks and handbasins must be clean and free-flowing to satisfy food hygiene regulations.
   • What hand washing facilities (separate from food preparation sinks) must also be available in the kitchen?

....

....

3   Work surfaces, tables and cutting boards must be kept clean at all times.
   • How should they be cleaned?

....

....

   • What are the dangers if they are not kept clean?

....

....

4 What protective clothing should be worn for cleaning tasks, and why?

....

5 Floors and walls must be clean and the floors kept dry.
  • What is the danger of a wet floor or if fat has been spilled?

....

....

6 Why should:

  a sink waste gullies be checked regularly and cleaned of any blockages?

....

  b traps used to collect tea leaves, grease and other debris be emptied and cleaned regularly?

....

  c shelves, cupboards and drawers be emptied and cleaned weekly?

....

7 Correct cleaning equipment and materials must be used. The cleaning specification should be supplied by your employer, but if ever in doubt about which, or how much, cleaning agent to use, what should you do?

....

8 Write out the correct procedure for the disposal of rubbish and waste food.

....

....

9 Why should rubbish not be allowed to accumulate outside a building?

....

....

10 Which is preferable: paper or plastic-lined bins which are destroyed with the rubbish, or unlined bins? Why?

....

....

11 What is a waste-master?

....

12 There are six good reasons why waste must be handled and disposed of correctly. Four of them are to comply with the law, to avoid creating a fire hazard, to prevent accidents, and to avoid pollution of the environment. Name the other two reasons:

....

....

13 Metal, painted and glass surfaces, floor and wall tiles, and vinyl or linoleum floor coverings must be cleaned to comply with health and safety legislation, food hygiene legislation and procedures laid down by your establishment.
   • Give three main reasons for cleaning, e.g. safeguard the quality of the finished products.

....

....

....

   • In catering there are two levels of cleanliness. One is physical cleanliness, the other is:

....

   • Name four factors which affect the quality of cleaning, e.g. temperature.

....

....

....

....

- State how you clean your food production areas after a training session or service.

....

....

....

....

14 Why should areas which are being cleaned be carefully marked?

....

15 Why should the cleaning of food production areas be carried out as soon as possible after use?

....

16 Why should cleaning equipment be stored separately from food items?

....

17 Why should detergents never be used in food areas?

....

18 Why should separate cleaning equipment be used for floors and work surfaces?

....

<u>1ND1.2</u> *Clean food production equipment*

Read pages 39–43 of *Practical Cookery.*

1 Food production equipment must be correctly turned off and dismantled before and during cleaning.
   - Why is this essential?

....

2 In order to satisfy health, safety and food regulation, equipment must be clean, dry and correctly re-assembled.

- Why is this essential, in particular with gas stoves?

....

3 Always use the correct cleaning equipment and materials as specified by your employer. Equipment must be correctly stored after cleaning.
   - How should saucepans be stored, and why?

....

4 Ovens, hobs, ranges, griddles, grids, salamanders, fryers, bainsmarie and hotplates must all be cleaned after each service in order to comply with health and safety legislation, food hygiene legislation and all relevant procedures laid down by your employer.
   - Why are people reluctant to clean equipment if it is difficult to re-assemble?

....

....

- Equipment should be so designed to protect the contents from external contamination. What does this mean?

....

....

- Equipment must be designed, constructed and finished to enable it to be

.... cleaned and ....
   - Every piece of large equipment should have laid-down procedures for cleaning. Choose one piece of large equipment in your establishment or training centre, write down the cleaning procedure for this piece of equipment.

   Name of equipment: ....

....

....

....

....

....

....

5 Why should faults and maintenance requirements be reported to the supervisor?

....

6 Why is it important to follow manufacturers' instructions when using cleaning materials and equipment?

....

7 What are the dangers of storing cleaning materials in incorrectly labelled containers?

....

8 Why should disinfectants never be used in food areas?

....

1ND1.3 *Clean food production utensils*

Read pages 41–43 of *Practical Cookery*.

1 What are the different procedures for cleaning, drying and storing of utensils?

....

....

2 Why should strainers and sieves be washed immediately after each use?

....

- If saucepans are difficult to clean, what is the best procedure to use before washing them?

....

- Why should scouring pads never be used on stainless steel?

....

- Why should wooden items never be allowed to soak in water?

....

3 Why is it important to follow manufacturers' instructions when using cleaning materials and equipment?

....

4 Why should cleaning materials always be stored in correctly labelled conainers?

....

5 Why should mechanical equipment be turned off before cleaning?

....

6 Why should equipment be dismantled before cleaning and correctly re-assembled after cleaning?

....

7 What extra care is required when cleaning teflon-coated items?

....

8 Draw a refuse compactor and label the working parts (if necessary, ask your tutor for help).

9 Cutting boards should be accepted on the basis of the following:
  a Water absorbency
  b Resistance to stains, cleaning chemicals, heat and food acids
  c Toxicity
  d Durability
  • What is is meant by toxicity and durability?

....

....

....

- Food utensils may be colour coded to assist in the cleaning procedure. What are the advantages of colour coding?

  ....

  ....

- How is small equipment washed and treated in your establishment or training centre?

  ....

  ....

  ....

  ....

- Does the kitchen where you are training have a sterilisation sink for food utensils? If the answer is yes, at what temperature does it operate?

  ....

- What purpose does washing-up liquid play in cleaning small kitchen utensils?

  ....

  ....

- Small utensils may cross-contaminate. What does this mean and how can it be avoided?

  ....

  ....

  ....

  ....

- Are you able to suggest ways in which small equipment could be better handled and treated in your establishment?

  ....

  ....

- Why does the following equipment cause specific cleaning problems?
a Conical strainer (chinois) ....
b Fine wooden sieve ....
c Manual can opener ....

Record of Achievement – Completion of Unit 1ND1

Candidate's signature: _____

Assessor's signature: _____

Date: _____

Handle and maintain knives

Read pages 26–32 of *Practical Cookery*.

1   Why is it important to keep knives clean and to satisfy food hygiene regulations?

....

2   Why is it important to keep knife blades sharp? To:

   a comply with food safety?

....

   b carry out knife work efficiently?

....

3   What are the dangers of working with blunt knives?

....

....

4   List the safety rules for knife handling.

....

....

....

5   How can cross contamination be prevented when using knives for different foods?

....

   • Set out a suggested colour coding for knife handles to be used for different foods.

....

....

6 Why is it important to select the correct knife for specific jobs:

    a from the safety point of view?

    ....

    b for working efficiently? Give examples.

    ....

    ....

7 Why should meat never be boned out or fish filleted from the frozen state?

    ....

8 What is the correct way to sharpen knife blades? What is the procedure for keeping them sharp at all times?

    ....

    ....

9 What are the essential requirements for stainless steel knives? What advantage have they over other knives?

    ....

    ....

Record of Achievement – Completion of Unit 1ND2

Candidate's signature: _____

Assessor's signature: _____

Date: _____

Maintain and promote hygiene in food storage, preparation and cooking

2ND22.1 *Contribute to food hygiene in food storage, preparation and cooking*

Read pages 43–56 of *Practical Cookery*, see also *Theory of Catering*, chapter on food storage.

1   Why is it essential to follow good hygiene practice at all times in the preparation, cooking and storage of food?

....

   • List three examples of bad practice that you have observed.

....

....

....

2   What are the appropriate operational procedures for reporting illness and infection?

....

....

3   What are an individual food handler's responsibilities under current food hygiene legislation?

....

4   Why is it important to check quality and freshness of food?

....

- Indicate signs of quality and freshness in the following:

- Whole plaice: ....

  Sirloin of beef: ....

  Brussel sprouts: ....

  Tomatoes: ....

5 Why is it important to thoroughly defrost food?

  ....

6 When cooked foods are not required for immediate consumption, why should they be cooled to room temperature before being stored?

  ....

7 What is the 'danger zone' and how does it affect bacteria?

  ....

8 What are the main types of bacteria and their associate foods?

  ....

  ....

  ....

9 What is cross contamination? What procedures must be followed to prevent cross contamination in the preparation and storage of food?

  ....

  ....

  ....

10 Why is it important to maintain personal hygiene when preparing, cooking and storing food?

  ....

- Give three examples of bad personal hygiene that you have observed.

....

....

....

11 Why are time and temperature important when preparing and cooking food?

....

- What are the potential dangers and effects?

....

12 List four unhygienic activities that a food handler may have to do after which it is essential that they wash their hands.

....

....

....

....

13 Name four checks to ensure that foodstuffs are in good hygiene condition on delivery.

....

....

....

....

14 Why is it important that unwashed and raw foods are kept separate from washed and cooked foods at key stages throughout processing?

....

15 Why is it essential to ensure that foods reach and are maintained at safe temperatures to comply with hygiene regulations throughout processing and service of foods?

....

• How can monitoring of temperature be carried out?

....

16   Why should hot foods which are to be stored for future use be cooled rapidly?

....

17   What is the correct way to defrost frozen foods?

....

• Why should frozen foods, e.g. whole chickens, be thoroughly defrosted before being cooked?

....

2ND22.2 *Clean and maintain hygiene in food storage, preparation and cooking*

Read pages 37–57 of *Practical Cookery.*

1   Why is it important to clean food production areas?

....

• How frequently should they be cleaned?

....

2   What do you understand by cross contamination?

....

....

• Give three examples of how cross contamination can occur.

....

....

....

3 What are the conditions for growth for germs?

....

....

• Give four examples of how germs can grow.

....

....

....

....

4 What are spores and toxins?

....

• Give examples of how spores and toxins can affect food.

....

....

5 List the animals that are legally considered pests.

....

....

....

....

....

6 Name the operational procedures that should be followed to minimise the risk of pest infestation.

....

....

....

Record of Achievement – Completion of Unit 2ND22

Candidate's signature: _____

Assessor's signature: _____

Date: _____

Unit 2ND1

Prepare and cook basic meat, poultry and offal dishes

2ND1.1 *Prepare basic meat, poultry and offal dishes*

Read pages 286–419 of *Practical Cookery*.

1 Why is it important to keep preparation areas, equipment and knives hygienic when preparing meat, poultry and offal?

....

• Give examples of unhygienic practices that you have observed.

....

2 What are the main contamination threats when preparing and storing uncooked meat?

....

3 List the quality and freshness points for:

Meat:

....

....

Poultry:

....

....

Offal:

....

....

4   Explain fully the following:

Contamination:

....

....

Pest infestation:

....

....

Cleanliness:

....

....

5   How can the skinning of poultry contribute to healthy eating practice?

....

6   How can the trimming of fat from meat contribute to healthy eating practice?

....

7   Why is it important to minimise salt added to meat, poultry and offal?

....

8   When preparing meat, poultry and offal dishes what additional ingredients can add fibre? Give two examples.

....

....

9   Preparation methods.
   • What is the purpose of trimming meat when preparing it for cooking?

....

- What should be done with the trimmings?

  ....

- Accepting that knives are clean, what else should be done to them before trimming and dicing meat?

  ....

- Name four dishes for which beef would be diced.

  ....

  ....

- When dicing meat, there are three important points to be borne in mind:

  Remove ....

  Cut ....

  Remove excess ....

- Which of the following meat joints are tied with string in order to retain their shape while cooking? Tick your answer(s).
  Best-end or rack of lamb
  7 lb joint of braised beef
  Boned stuffed shoulder of lamb
  10 lb of beef topside

- What is the reason for rolling certain meat joints?

  ....

- Name two joints that can be prepared by rolling.

  ....

- Stuffing of certain meat joints is a means of adding extra flavour, seasoning and variety. Name three meat joints suitable for stuffing.

  ....

  ....

- List the ingredients of a suitable stuffing for each of the three meat joints:

  ....

  ....

- After stuffing a meat joint, what else must be done before it is ready for cooking and why?

  ....

- Certain cuts of meat are batted either to: get them to a required shape; get them to a required thickness or thinness; or to tenderise them. What veal cut would be batted out thinly?

  ....

- For what beef or veal dish would lean slices of beef or veal be batted out thinly?

  ....

- Barding is the covering of certain lean, tender pieces or joints of meat with thin slices of fat bacon before cooking. What is the purpose of a bard?

  ....

- Why is it essential to tie a bard in place before cooking?

  ....

- Name two joints or cuts of meat that might be barded.

  ....

- What is the correct method of preparing wing rib of beef for roasting? (Give your answer, then check it with page 330, *Practical Cookery.*)

  ....

  ....

10 Food hygiene.
   - There are eight main contamination threats when preparing and storing uncooked meat. Four are concerned with the transfer of food poisoning bacteria. Describe these in detail.

  ....

....

....

....

- The remaining four are concerned with: uncovered food; disposal and storage; storage temperatures; and thawing procedures.
  Describe each of these in detail.

....

....

....

....

- Give two reasons why preparation work must be planned and sufficient time allocated to meet daily schedules.

....

....

- If the meat ordered is not of the correct type, quality and quantity required, what could be the result in each case?
  Incorrect type, e.g. beef chuck steak for beef olives:

....

....

Cheapest quality:

....

....

Incorrect quantity:

....

....

- Why is it important to ensure that not only the correct equipment is used, but also the correct size of equipment? Give two examples and reasons.

....

....

11 Preparation of beef (page 325, *Practical Cookery*).
- How is beef assessed for quality?

....

- Name three beef joints suitable for roasting.

....

- What are the three essential points of preparation required for a joint of beef to be roasted?

....

....

....

- What is the traditional joint of beef used for boiling and how is it prepared?

....

....

....

- What thickness is rump steak cut for steaks?

....

- Why is a minute steak so called, from what beef joint is it cut and how is it prepared?

....

....

....

- What is the difference in the preparation between a joint of beef for boiling English style and French style?

....

....

12 Preparation of veal (page 358, *Practical Cookery*).
   - From which joint of veal are the best escalopes cut?

....

   - Describe the preparation of a veal escalope for Viennoise?

....

   - How is the meat prepared for a veal sauté?

....

   - How is a breast of veal prepared for roasting?

....

   - What is the difference in preparation of the meat for a fricassée and a blanquette of veal?

....

....

13 Preparation of lamb and mutton (page 298, *Practical Cookery*).
   - When preparing lamb and mutton joints, why are some or all bones sometimes removed?

....

....

   - How is a quality lamb carcass assessed?

....

   - How many bones are there in a shoulder of lamb?

....

- What is the difference between lamb and mutton?

  ....

- Describe the preparation of a loin of lamb for stuffing and roasting.

  ....

  ....

- What is the difference between a loin chop and a Barnsley chop?
  What could be another name for a Barnsley chop?

  ....

  ....

- Describe the preparation of a best-end (rack) of lamb for roasting.

  ....

- Name three boneless cuts of lamb.

  ....

- How is meat prepared for a hot-pot?

  ....

14 Preparation of pork (page 375, *Practical Cookery*).
- What are the four quality points for pork?

  ....

  ....

- What is meant by 'scoring a joint of pork'?

  ....

- What herb is traditionally used for seasoning a boned belly of pork before rolling?

  ....

• How is meat prepared for sweet and sour pork?

....

15 Preparation of bacon (page 385, *Practical Cookery*).
• Name the five bacon joints and give an example of use for each joint.

....

....

....

....

• What are the five signs of quality in a side of bacon?

....

....

....

....

• What are the two ways of preparing a hock of bacon for boiling?

....

....

• Why is it usually necessary to soak bacon joints before boiling?

....

• What is the name of the bone in a gammon which will hinder carving if it is not removed?

....

16 Preparation of offal (page 291, *Practical Cookery*).
• What basic preparation is required for beef, lamb, veal and pigs' kidneys?

....

- How are kidneys prepared for sauté?

....

- How is lamb, veal and pigs' liver prepared for cooking?

....

....

- What is the preparation for lamb and veal sweetbreads?

....

....

....

- How are lamb, veal and ox tongues prepared?

....

....

....

- How is tripe prepared for cooking?

....

....

....

17 Preparation of poultry (pages 389–397, *Practical Cookery*)

18 The term poultry is applied to all domestic fowl used for food: chicken, turkeys, ducks, geese and pigeons.
   - What is the difference between a battery-reared and free-range chicken?

....

19 Preparation methods.

a Washing: before preparing poultry for cooking whole, the insides must be checked for cleanliness and washed thoroughly under cold running water if necessary.
- Why is this so important?

....

b Skinning: for certain dishes, e.g. supremes, kebabs, the skin is removed by pulling it off firmly with the fingers and carefully cutting any holding sinews if necessary.
- For what purposes are chicken skinned in your establishment?

....

c Trimming: it is usual to trim chicken pieces in order to neaten the shape. In older fowls it may be necessary to remove fat.
- What are chicken trimmings of skin and bone used for?

....

d Jointing (pages 393–4, *Practical Cookery*).
- In to how many pieces is a 1¼ kg (2½ lb) chicken usually cut for sauté?

....

....

e Trussing or tieing (pages 392–3, *Practical Cookery*).
- Before trussing a chicken or turkey for roasting, why is it sensible to remove the wishbone?

....

f Batting: when preparing suprêmes of chicken and escalopes of chicken or turkey, a meat bat and a little water may be used to help give shape or/and thinness.
g Barding: a bard is a thin slice of fat bacon which is used to cover the tender parts (breasts) of birds before roasting. The bard should be tied on with string.
h Dicing: for certain dishes of chicken and turkey, e.g. stir-fry kebabs, the birds are skinned and all the bones are removed and the meat neatly diced. The white and dark meat should be kept separately.
- Why should the white and dark meat be kept separate?

....

51

i What is a marinade?

....

• Give two examples of marinades used for chicken.

....

....

20 Food hygiene.
   • What is cross contamination and why is it so essential to take all possible steps to avoid it when preparing poultry?

....

....

....

• What is salmonella?

....

• Salmonella is present in approximately 20, 40, or 60% of raw and frozen chicken?

....

• Why should fresh uncooked chicken and cooked roast chicken not be stored together?

....

• What is the danger of using the same preparation areas, equipment and utensils for preparing cooked and uncooked poultry?

....

• What is another name for bacteria?

....

• What is the danger to health if unhygienic equipment, utensils and preparation methods are used when handling poultry.

....

- What examples of unhygienic equipment and preparation methods have you seen, and what would be your remedy?

  ....

  ....

21 Pests.
- How can rats, mice, flies, cockroaches and other vermin contaminate uncovered food?

  ....

22 Storage.
- What is the correct way to store waste and unused food items from the kitchen? What are the dangers if this is not done correctly?

  ....

  ....

23 Thawing.
- What are the main contamination dangers of storing poultry at incorrect temperatures and incorrect thawing procedures when using frozen poultry?

  ....

  ....

- What is the correct way to defrost frozen chicken?

  ....

  ....

- If chicken suprêmes are required to be prepared for lunch and frozen chicken are delivered at 10 am, what is likely to happen?

  ....

  ....

  ....

- What examples, if any, of inefficiency have you observed in the use and preparation of poultry?

....

....

....

24 Preparation of chicken (page 391–5, *Practical Cookery*).
   - List four signs of quality in chicken.

....

....

   - What is meant by eviscerating?

....

   - What is a suitable weight of chicken for cutting for sauté?

....

   - Briefly describe the preparation of a chicken for grilling?

....

   - What is a suitable weight of chicken for suprêmes?

....

   - Why are the fillets lifted from suprêmes? What then happens to them?

....

   - How is a chicken ballotine prepared?

....

   - Draw a chicken prepared for spatchcock.

2ND1.2 *Cook basic meat, poultry and offal dishes*

1 At all times before, during and after cooking, the following points must be borne in mind:

a Cooking areas and equipment are ready for use and satisfy health, safety and hygiene regulations;

b Work is planned and sufficient time is allocated to meet daily schedules;

c Meat or poultry is cooked according to customer and recipe requirements;

d Meat and poultry dishes are finished and presented according to customer and dish requirements;

e Preparation and cooking areas and equipment are correctly cleaned after use;

f If any unexpected situation should occur, appropriate action must be taken within the individual's responsibility;

g All work should be carried out in an organised and efficient manner taking account of priorities and laid-down procedures.

2 What are the main contamination threats when cooking and storing meat, poultry and offal dishes?

....

• Give examples of bad practice that you have observed.

....

3 Why is it important to keep cooking areas and equipment and knives clean and hygienic?

....

4 Why are time and temperature important when cooking meat, poultry and offal dishes? Give two examples to illustrate your answer.

....

....

5 What cooking methods and equipment can contribute to reduced fat in cooked meat, poultry and offal dishes?

....

• Give two examples for meat and one each for poultry and offal.

....

....

6   Why is it important to follow safe working practices when cooking with fats/oils?

....

   •   Tabulate the safe working practices.

7   What do you understand by the 'flash point'?

....

   •   What are the signs to look for when fat/oil is approaching flash point?

....

   •   What procedure should be followed if fat/oil reaches flash point?

....

8   How can the fibre content of a recipe be increased when cooking meat, poultry and offal dishes?

....

   •   Give an example for one meat, one poultry and one offal dish.

....

....

9   Why is it important to minimise salt added to meat, poultry and offal dishes?

....

10 Roasting (pages 91–94, *Practical Cookery*).
- Describe the two methods of roasting and their variations.

....

....

- Name the important points in making a roast gravy.

....

- How is roast gravy made in your establishment and, if it is different from the traditional method, why is this so?

....

....

....

- Which are the only two meats which are sometimes cooked and served pink?

....

....

- When cooking roast beef, what fat should be used to make Yorkshire puddings and why?

....

....

- When roasting pork, how can the crackling be made crisp?

....

- When roasting veal, how can the flavour be increased during the cooking?

....

- What is the traditional difference between roast gravy for beef and veal?

....

- Why should roast chickens be cooked on their sides rather than with the breasts uppermost?

....

- How is a roast chicken tested to see if it is cooked?

....

- Why is frequent basting recommended when roasting meat or poultry?

....

- What are the five important points to be observed when roasting?

....

....

....

....

....

- Complete the following table:

	Approximate cooking times	Degree of cooking
Beef	...... min per ½ kg (1 lb) and ...... min over	Underdone
Lamb	...... min per ½ kg (1 lb) and ...... min over	Cooked through
Lamb	...... min per ½ kg (1 lb) and ...... min over	Cooked pink
Mutton	...... min per ½ kg (1 lb) and ...... min over	Cooked through
Veal	...... min per ½ kg (1 lb) and ...... min over	Cooked through
Pork	...... min per ½ kg (1 lb) and ...... min over	Thoroughly cooked

Insert the required cooking times for each of these meats.
- Approximate roasting times for chicken or turkey are 15–20 minutes per lb. True or false?

....

- What is a meat thermometer? What is its purpose?

....

- Why are roast joints set on a trivet in the roasting tray?

....

- Name two types of trivet.

....

....

- Without the use of a meat thermometer, how can meat be tested to ensure it is cooked through?

....

- Why is it important to time the cooking of roasts in order to let them rest after they are cooked and before carving?

....

....

- Why is it important to carefully conserve the meat sediment in a roasting tray after the joint is used?

....

11 Grilling (page 96, *Practical Cookery*).
- Name three methods of grilling and give the variations in each case.

....

....

....

- Why must grills be pre-heated and lightly oiled prior to use?

....

- Complete the first column in the following table:

Degrees of cooking grilled meats		Appearance of juice issuing from the meat when pressed
....	Rare	Red and bloody
....	Underdone	Reddish pink
....	Just done	Pink
....	Well done	Clear

Insert the missing words to describe the degree of cooking.

- Name four items which when grilling under the salamander it is sensible to put on trays. Why?

  ....

  ....

  ....

  ....

- Give four general rules for efficient grilling.

  ....

  ....

  ....

  ....

- List four safety rules when grilling.

  ....

  ....

  ....

  ....

- Name four combinations of food suitable for cooking as kebabs.
  Lamb ....
  Peppers ....
  Monk fish ....

  ....

- Name two suggestions for marinades for kebabs.

  ....

  ....

- On a bed of what are kebabs usually served?

....

- What is the final finish for devilled grilled chicken?

....

12 Describe barbecuing, and give example of various foods that can be cooked by this method.

....

....

....

13 Tandoori cooking is named after the unusual clay oven called the *tandoor,* which produces slightly charred spiced chicken and lamb dishes. Tandoor meats are first marinaded to flavour and tenderise them; many of the marinades contain a red colouring agent. Foods to be cooked are placed on long spits and positioned vertically inside the oven. The meats are first seared with high heat, then the marinade is applied repeatedly and allowed to dry on the surface, leaving a residue that forms a crust and seals the juices in the meat.

      If a traditional tandoor is not available then an oven grill, rôtisserie or barbecue can be used provided the basic rules and principles of tandoori cooking are applied.

14 Shallow frying (page 99, *Practical Cookery*).
      When shallow frying foods, why should the presentation side be fried first?

....

- What is the difference between a frying and a sauté pan?

....

- Why is correctly deglazing a pan after frying meat or poultry so important?

....

- Describe the deglazing process in detail.

....

....

- Describe the difference between a sauté of beef and a ragoût of beef.

....

....

- What pre-preparation is required for a griddle before using it for cooking?

....

- Name four foods that may be cooked on a griddle.

....

....

- What is stir frying? ....

....

- What is the traditional pan used for stir frying? ....
- What substitute for the traditional stir fry pan can be used?

....

- Ask your tutor or trainer why the Chinese developed stir fry.
- Name a popular cut of lamb that is shallow fried and the type of pan traditionally used.

....

- When cooking a sauté of kidneys, why are the kidneys drained in a colander after they are cooked and the drained off liquid discarded?

....

- Why should kidneys not be re-boiled after being sautéed, drained and placed in a sauce?

....

- Name two liquids which may be used to deglaze a pan in which kidneys have been fried.

....

- When cooking a chicken sauté, why are the leg pieces cooked for a little longer that the breast pieces?

15 Braising (page 83, *Practical Cookery*).
  - What is the essential difference between braising and roasting meat?

  ....

  - What are the two basic methods of braising (give an example of meat or poultry cooked by each).

  ....

  - What is the first cooking procedure when braising meat, and why is the procedure necessary?

  ....

  - Describe why braising is a suitable method of cookery for less tender joints of meat.

  ....

  - Give two advantages of braising meats and poultry.

  ....

  ....

  - Should cooking liquid for braising boil rapidly, boil steadily, simmer gently or barely simmer? ....
  Give the reasons why for your answer.

  ....

  ....

  - What type of pans or oven-proof dishes should be used for braising?

  ....

  - Once a joint has come to the boil, what is an ideal oven temperature for cooking?

  ....

  - Name a piece of large equipment suitable for braising in large-scale catering.

  ....

- Describe how braised joints of meat can be glazed.

  ....

- What other ingredients are added to a joint of beef to be braised?

  ....

- When braising a joint, how far up should liquid be added?

  ....

- Name two joints of beef suitable for braising.

  ....

- Why have you chosen these two joints?

  ....

  ....

- How are vegetables prepared before they are added to a braised joint?

  ....

- When serving, should braised beef be cut in thick or thin slices?

  ....

- Name two suitable garnishes for braised beef.

  ....

- How thick should steaks for braising be cut?

  ....

- Name a traditional sauce served with braised ox tongue.

  ....

- What is a popular vegetable cooked in and served with ox liver?

  ....

- What is the usual pre-preparation for braised shoulder of veal?

....

- When braising a duck with peas, what two other ingredients are usually added as part of the garnish?

....

16 Stewing (page 81, *Practical Cookery*).
   - Give the definition for stewing.

....

- Why is stewing suitable for cheaper cuts of meat and poultry?

....

- Name three ways in which stews can be thickened.

....

- What are the two ways in which stews may be cooked?

....

....

- What is the effect of the stewing process on meat?

....

....

- What is the ideal cooking temperature for stewing? How could you describe it without giving figures?

....

- If a hot pan is taken out of the oven, how can it be marked as a warning to others that it is hot?

....

- What is the traditional Hungarian dish of stewed beef with paprika called?

....

- What is the traditional garnish for this dish?

....

- What is the name given to a dish of chicken pieces cooked in a white sauce?

....

- What would be a typical garnish to this dish?

....

- How should a liaison be used in this dish and what is its purpose?

....

- What is tripe?

....

- What is an approximate cooking time for tripe and onions?

....

- Name three different ways of thickening a dish of tripe.

....

....

....

17   Boiling (page 77, *Practical Cookery*).
- Name four liquids in which foods can be boiled.

....

....

- Why, when boiling meats, is it important to boil gently?

....

- What is another name for boiling gently?

....

- What would be the difference in the texture of meat if a joint is allowed to boil quickly rather than gently?

....

- What are the advantages of starting to boil food in cold liquid, brought to the boil and allowed to boil gently?

....

- What are the advantages of adding food to boiling liquid, re-boiling and allowing to boil gently?

....

- Why is it important to skim the surface of the liquid frequently during the boiling of meat or poultry?

....

- In addition to carrots and onions, what is the traditional ingredient cooked in and served with silverside of beef?

....

- What is the difference between beef boiled English and French style?

....

- Should silverside of beef be carved with or against the grain?

....

- What is the approximate cooking time per lb for boiled beef?

....

- What other ingredients are added when boiling a chicken?

....

- Name a suitable sauce served with boiled chicken.

  ....

- Name and describe the method of producing the traditional accompaniment to boiled chicken.

  ....

  ....

  ....

- How is a boiled chicken tested to ensure that it is cooked?

  ....

Record of Achievement – Completion of Unit 2ND1

Candidate's signature: _____

Assessor's signature: _____

Date: _____

Unit 2ND2

Prepare and cook basic fish dishes

2ND2.1 *Prepare fish for cooking*

Read pages 242–254 of *Practical Cookery*.

1   What are the main contamination threats when preparing and storing uncooked fish?

   ....

   • Give examples of any bad practice that you have observed.

   ....

2   What are the dangers if preparation, cooking and storage areas and equipment are not kept hygienic?

   ....

   • State examples of any bad practice that you may have observed.

   ....

3   Why should cooked food not for immediate consumption be cooled rapidly or maintained at a safe hot temperature after cooking? Give examples.

   ....

   ....

4   Why is it important to use knives that are a suitable shape for the task, and clean and hygienic?

   ....

5   Why should frozen fish be thoroughly defrosted before cooking?

   ....

- What is the correct way to defrost frozen fish?

  ....

6 List the quality points of fresh fish.

  ....

7 Which preparation methods can be used to increase the fibre of a finished dish?

  ....

8 For healthy eating, which are the fats to use for cooking?

  ....

9 What is the contribution of fish to a healthy diet?

  ....

10 Which types of fish and coatings minimise fat in a dish?

  ....

11 Before considering fish preparation, the following points need to be understood and carried out:
  a Preparation areas and equipment are ready for use and satisfy health, safety and hygiene regulations.
  b Work is planned and appropriate time is allocated to meet schedules.
  c Fish is of the correct type, quality and quantity.
  d Fish is correctly prepared according to dish requirements.
  e Where appropriate, prepared fish is combined with other ingredients ready for cooking.
  f Appropriate equipment for cooking is ready for use.
  g Preparation areas and equipment are correctly cleaned after use.
  h All work is carried out in an organised and efficient manner.
  - Name four round and four flat fish.

  ....

  ....

12 Fish may be delivered either:
  a whole, uncleaned and certain fish, e.g. salmon, with the scales on;

b whole, cleaned (gutted) but with the head and scales on;

c filleted, with or without skins.

- Irrespective of the type of fish and the way it is to be prepared why is careful washing and draining essential?

....

13 With most fish, trimming of some kind is required. If the fish is to be served whole, then the scales must be removed, the fins are cut off using fish scissors and, if the head is to be left on, the gills and eyes are removed.

14 Fish fillets need to be checked for any bones that may remain and any discoloured parts cut away.
- Is it necessary to remove the head of plaice before filleting? ....
- When filleting flat fish, do you work from head to tail or from tail to head?

....

- Do you start on the back or belly side when filleting round fish?

....

15 Portioning (page 248, *Practical Cookery*).
- What is an approximate weight of fish per portion, on the bone and off the bone?

....

16 Baking (page 253, *Practical Cookery*).
- Name three fish or cuts of fish that are suitable for stuffing.

....

- Suggest a suitable stuffing for each.

....

....

17 Hygiene.
- What are the main contamination threats when storing raw fish?

....

....

....

- What is the main threat from storing fish at incorrect temperatures?

....

- What is the threat from thawing frozen fish incorrectly?

....

- What is the contamination threat from unclean fish?

....

2ND2.2 *Cook fish dishes*

1 Before any cooking starts, the following points need to be observed (enlarge on the importance of each):

  a Preparation and cooking areas and equipment are ready and satisfy health, safety and hygiene regulations.

....

  b Work is planned and time is allocated to meet daily schedules.

....

  c Fish dishes are correctly cooked and presented according to customer requirements.

....

  d Preparation and cooking areas and equipment are correctly cleaned after use.

....

  e All work is carried out in an organised and efficient manner.

....

2 Baking (page 252, *Practical Cookery*).
  - Describe a method of baking a whole fish, e.g. a sea bass 400 g (1 lb) weight.

....

- Describe how you would stuff and bake 48 portions of cod.

....

....

- Describe how you would stuff and bake fillets of plaice.

....

3 Grilling (page 251, *Practical Cookery*).
   - Describe the preparation of fish for grilling.

....

- What is the test to ensure that grilled darnes of cod or salmon are cooked?

....

- Before grilling a whole fish, e.g. herring, what preparation is carried out to ensure that it cooks through?

....

- What are the three different ways of grilling fish?

....

- What is the traditional sauce served with grilled herring?

....

- How can the preparation of mackerel for grilling differ from herring?

....

- After grilling whole plaice, which side is presented to the customer?

....

- Before grilling Dover soles and plaice, why do you only remove the black skin from the soles?

....

4 Frying (pages 99–105 and 251, *Practical Cookery*).
   - What is the difference between shallow fried fish and fish shallow fried meunière?

....

- Before slicing lemon for garnish meunière, why is it important to remove the peel and pith, and then the pips?

  ....

- Why is it important to cook the presentation side of shallow fried fish first?

  ....

- Would it be incorrect to shallow fry and serve fish without the meunière finish?

  ....

- How can you tell when butter is cooked to the nut brown (beurre noisette) stage?

  ....

- If required to cook turbot or brill meunière, how would you cut the fish?

  ....

- Given the choice of serving four portions of fillets of plaice meunière on a silver flat or plates, which would you choose and why?

  ....

- Suggest three suitable accompaniments for deep fried fish.

  ....

5   Fried fish (page 261, *Practical Cookery*).
   - What is an essential requirement for a fat or oil to be suitable for deep frying?

     ....

   - What will happen to the food being fried if the frying medium smokes at a low temperature?

     ....

   - Why must any frying medium be free from moisture?

     ....

- With regard to frying, what do you understand by 'flash point'?

....

- Name four points that indicate when a frying medium should be discarded.

....

....

....

- Why is fish coated before being deep fried?

....

- Name three different ways of coating fish before deep frying?

....

....

....

- Before deep frying fillets of plaice, both white and black skins should be removed.

    True or false? ....

- Would there be any difference in the frying temperature for cooking fried sole, goujons of plaice and whitebait and, if so, why?

....

- Describe the preparation, cooking and serving of whitebait.

....

6 Poaching (page 250, *Practical Cookery*).
   - Why is it important when poaching fish, to keep the amount of liquid to the minimum?

....

• Name four liquids in which fish can be poached.

....

....

• What fish is usually poached in milk?

....

• Describe the procedure for making a sauce from the cooking liquid after fish have been poached. ....

....

• When poaching fish, why is time and temperature control so important?

....

• Turbot may be poached whole, cut in slices on the bone or in portions off the bone. Give the correct name and a way in which it could appear on a menu for:

a a slice of turbot on the bone: ....

b a portion of turbot off the bone: ....

• Describe the method of poaching and serving slices of turbot on the bone. ....

....

• Does the method of poaching slices of halibut cod or brill on the bone differ from turbot and, if so, how?

....

• What is the term used for a slice of salmon on the bone, and what is the most suitable sized fish from which to cut slices?

....

• What is a court-bouillon? Give a suitable recipe and name the fish it is usually connected with.

....

....

- Suggest two suitable sauces to accompany hot poached salmon.

  ....

- Describe the cooking and finish of skate with black butter.

  ....

  ....

- Describe the preparation and cooking of fish cakes.

  ....

  ....

7 Steaming (pages 86–88 and 251, *Practical Cookery*).
- All fish which is poached or boiled may be steamed. True or false?

  ....

- Describe low pressure, high pressure and sous-vide methods of steaming.

  ....

  ....

  ....

  ....

- What are the advantages of sous-vide cookery?

  ....

  ....

  ....

- What is the name given to the detailed preparation, cooking and serving of a suitable fish dish cooked sous-vide?

  ....

- What is an essential safety precaution to observe before opening a steamer door after use?

....

Record of Achievement – Completion of Unit 2ND2

Candidate's signature: _____

Assessor's signature: _____

Date: _____

Prepare and cook basic cold and hot desserts

2ND3.1 *Prepare, cook and finish basic cold desserts*

Read pages 586 and 594–602 of *Practical Cookery*.

1 Give three points of quality and freshness for eggs.

    ....

    ....

    ....

2 Draw and explain in words what happens to the white and yolk of an egg if it is kept for too long.

3 Why should eggs not be stored near strong smelling foods, such as cheese, onions and fish?

    ....

    • In how many sizes are hens' eggs available?

    ....

    • What is salmonella infection and how can it be passed into hens' eggs?

    ....

    • With regard to the dangers of salmonella infection, what is the advantage of using pasteurised egg and in how many forms is pasteurised egg available?

    ....

    ....

- Most salmonella infections cause only a mild stomach upset, but the effects can be serious on two types of the population. Name these.

  ....

- Does the pasteurisation of eggs affect their keeping or ingredient quality?

  ....

4 When cooking a fresh egg and milk mixture, it is essential to cook over a gentle heat and stir continuously.

  a Why?

  ....

  b Once the eggs and milk mixture has cooked and thickened, is it necessary to remove it from the heat and, if so, why?

  ....

5 After cooking an eggs and milk mixture, why is it essential to strain the mixture through a fine strainer?

  ....

6 If a cooked mixture of eggs and milk is removed from the heat and left in the pan without stirring, what will happen?

  ....

7 When making pastry cream, after having whisked on the boiling milk to the remainder of the ingredients, why is it necessary to clean the pan before returning the mixture and completing the cooking?

  ....

8 When pastry cream is removed into a container, how can the forming of a skin on top be prevented?

  ....

9 Hygiene.
  - What are the main contamination threats when storing, preparing and cooking egg mixtures in relation to:

a   Using the same preparation areas, equipment and utensils for preparing cooked and uncooked products:

....

b   Using unhygienic equipment, utensils and preparation methods (support your answer with examples):

....

....

c   Touching the mouth, nose, open cuts, sores and unclean hands then handling food:

....

d   Uncovered foods and pests:

....

e   Incorrect disposal of waste:

....

f   Incorrect storage of unused items:

....

10   Give four reasons why it is important to keep preparation and cooking areas and equipment hygienic.

....

....

....

....

11   Time and temperature are important when cooking egg-based desserts to ensure they are correctly cooked, to prevent food poisoning, and to minimise loss of nutritional value from prepared food.

- Give any examples where you have seen incorrect practice of the above three points.

   ....

   ....

   ....

12   The following are basic preparation methods associated with cold desserts. Give an example of a cold dessert produced from each preparation method.

Preparation method	Cold dessert
Piping	....
Mixing	....
Aeration	Cold lemon souffle
Combining	....
Addition of flavours/colours	....
Puréeing	....

13   Name four fruits suitable for cold poached fruits that can be served as a cold dessert garnish.

   ....

   ....

14   Name a dessert produced in each of the following categories.

Category	Cold dessert
Trifle	Whisky trifle
Egg custard	....
Cold rice dessert	....
Flans	Apple flan
Basic meringue	....

Moulded creams ....

Fruit based ....

15 Why is meringue classified as a foam? What effect does cream of tartar have on egg white?

....

....

16 Assess the quality points of the following cold desserts.

Cold dessert	Texture	Flavour	Aroma	Appearance	Consistency
Strawberry meringue nest					
Caramel cream					
Fresh fruit salad					
Gooseberry flan					
Raspberry mousse					
Rice condé					

17 List the fruits suitable for a tropical fruit salad.

....

....

....

18 Name two cold desserts produced by each of the following cooking methods.

Boiling: ....

Stewing: ....

Poaching: ....

Baking: ....

19 Name a cold dessert produced using the following finishing methods, briefly describing each method.

Finishing method	Explanation	Cold dessert
Cooling	Rapid reduction in temperature	
Glazing		
Filling		
Piping		
Demoulding	Remove from mould	Chocolate mousse
Dusting		
Chilling		

20 When preparing cold desserts it is essential to observe strict hygiene and safe working practices. Why?

....

21 What are the main contamination threats to be aware of when preparing, cooking and storing basic cold desserts?

....

....

22 State why time and temperature is important when:

a preparing cold desserts:

....

b cooking cold desserts:

....

c cooling cold desserts:

....

d finishing cold desserts:

....

23 Name a different cold dessert which may be produced from each of the following fruits.

Apple...

Mango..

Pear...

Passion fruit ....

24 From some of the following ingredients, name three cold desserts which may be produced, listing the ingredients used in each case.

short pastry	breadcrumbs
puff pastry	cake crumbs
eggs	couverture
apples	glacé fruits
caster sugar/icing sugar	fresh oranges
milk	bananas
cornflour	Carolina rice
plain flour	sultanas
fresh whipping cream	

• State the quality points you would look for in each of your chosen cold desserts.

....

....

....

• Sketch your suggested plate presentation for one of your named cold desserts.

25 List a selection of six cold desserts suitable for a Brasserie menu.

....

....

....

26 Suggest two cold desserts suitable for a banquet of 500 people.

....

27 List any problems that are likely to occur when preparing these desserts in large quantities.

....

....

2ND3.2 *Prepare and finish basic hot desserts*

1 List the ingredients for 200 g (8 oz) of pancake batter.

....

....

....

• List four fillings for pancakes.

....

....

....

....

2 Suggest a suitable hot dessert for each of the following categories:

Category	Hot dessert
Sponge	....
Egg custard	....
Cereals	Semolina pudding
Fruit	....
Pies	....
Pancakes	....

3 Suggest two hot desserts which may be produced from each of the following basic preparation methods:

a creaming:

....

....

b aeration:

....

....

c moulding:

....

....

4 Assess the quality points of the following hot desserts:

Hot dessert	Texture	Appearance	Flavour	Aroma	Consistency
Chocolate souffle			Rich in chocolate	Freshly baked chocolate	
Steamed sponge pudding					
Steamed treacle pudding					
Creamed rice pudding	smooth and creamy	white identifiable rice grains			
Pineapple fritters	crisp fruit, soft				
Steamed jam roll					
Mincemeat tart					

5 State the differences between a soufflé and a soufflé pudding.

....

....

6 From the following preparation methods name a hot dessert which may be produced.

Preparation method	Hot dessert
Folding	....
	....
Mixing	....
	....
Peeling	Apples Apple fritters
Portioning	....
	....
Slicing	....
	....
Filling	....
	....

7 Name a hot dessert produced from the following cooking methods:

boiling: ....

poaching: ....

steaming: steamed lemon sponge pudding

baking: ....

bain marie: ....

combination cooking: ....

8   Name a hot dessert produced using the following finishing methods:

Finishing method	Hot dessert
Filling	....
Dusting	....
Glazing	....
Portioning	....
Demoulding	Soufflé pudding

9   It is important to observe strict hygienic and safe working practices when preparing, cooking and finishing basic hot desserts. Why?

....

10   What are the main contamination threats to be aware of when preparing, cooking and finishing basic hot desserts?

....

11   Why should hot desserts be maintained at a safe hot temperature after cooking? What should this temperature be?

12   List six hot sweets suitable to serve at lunch in an industrial staff restaurant catering for both manual and office workers.

....

....

....

• How should each be portioned and served, using counter service?

....

....

13 Suggest a hot dessert which may be produced from the following fruits:

Comice pears: ....

Bramley apples: ....

Cherries: ....

Gooseberries: ....

Raspberries: ....

Record of Achievement – Completion of Unit 2ND3

Candidate's signature: _____

Assessor's signature: _____

Date: _____

Unit 2ND4

Prepare and cook basic stocks, sauces and soups

2ND4.1 *Prepare and cook basic stocks*

Read pages 111–115 of *Practical Cookery*.

1 As stocks are the foundation of many important kitchen preparations, the greatest possible care should be taken in their production (page 111, *Practical Cookery*).
   a Preparation and cooking areas and equipment before being used must satisfy health, safety and hygiene regulations.
   b Work should be planned and appropriate time allowed to meet daily schedules, e.g. if a stock takes six hours to cook, it is bad planning to start it three hours before the end of a day's work.
   c Ingredients are of the correct type, sound in quality and sufficient quantity.
   d Ingredients are correctly prepared and cooked according to the recipes.
   e Cooked stock, if not to be used immediately, is correctly and safely stored according to food hygiene legislation.
   f Preparation and cooking areas and equipment are correctly cleaned after use.

2 Why are stocks such a high risk product?

   ....

3 List the main contamination threats when preparing, cooking and storing stocks.

   ....

4 Why is it important to keep preparation and cooking areas and equipment hygienic?

   ....

   • List any bad practices that you may have observed with regard to stocks.

   ....

   ....

- Give two reasons why unsound meat or bones and decaying vegetables should not be used for stock.

  ....

  ....

- If scum is not removed during cooking it will boil into the stock and spoil the colour and ....
- If stock is allowed to boil rather than gently simmer, it will evaporate and ....
- What is the danger of allowing stock to go off the boil, particularly in hot weather?

  ....

  ....

- Why should salt not be added to stock?

  ....

- If stock is to be kept, there are four procedures to be carried out, straining, reboiling and ....

5 When making chicken stock, if chicken carcasses are not available, what can be used as a substitute?

   ....

6 General methods for white and brown stocks (pages 113–115, *Practical Cookery*).

   a When chopping beef bones for stock, why is any fat or marrow removed and what safety precautions should be observed?

      ....

      ....

   b To help keep a meat or game stock clean, blanching and refreshing is necessary. How is this done?

      ....

      ....

      ....

c Just before stock comes to the boil, if a good measure of cold water is added it will help to throw the scum and fat to the surface and ....

d What is the approximate cooking time for a beef stock?

....

e The three ingredients in a bouquet garni for beef stock are:

....

• The outside leaves of which vegetable are often used to enclose a bouquet garni?

....

• How could you describe a bouquet garni in English?

....

f To make a brown beef stock, the bones are browned well on all sides either by placing in a roasting tin in the oven or ....
• Before placing the browned bones in the stock pot, what must be done with them?

....

g Deglazing is an important procedure that follows the removal of the browned bones from the tray. What is the purpose of deglazing and how is it done?

....

....

....

....

h Why are the roughly chopped vegetables also coloured for brown stock?

....

i In addition to squashed (but sound) tomatoes, what other ingredient may be added to brown stock?

....

j If it takes 6–8 hours to extract the flavour from beef bones, how long should it take for a chicken stock made from raw carcasses: 1–2 hours, 3–4 hours or 5–6 hours? ....

7 Fish stock (page 114, *Practical Cookery*).
  • Why does fish stock only require 20 minutes cooking time?

  ....

  • What would be the effect on the flavour of cooking fish stock for 1 hour?

  ....

  • Why is it essential that fish bones used for stock are well washed and perfectly fresh?

  ....

8 Vegetarian stocks (pages 114–115, *Practical Cookery*).
  • Give four suitable vegetables for making vegetable stock.

  ....

  • What approximate length of cooking time is required for vegetable stock: ½ hour, 1 hour, 1½ hours or 2 hours? ....
  • When making brown vegetable stock, why is it not suitable to colour off ingredients using lard or dripping?

  ....

  • For what type of dishes are vegetable stocks used?

  ....

9 There are many possibilities of contamination when preparing, cooking and storing stocks.
  a If raw and cooked ingredients are *stored* together, e.g. cooked stock and raw bones or strong smelling vegetables.
  b Using the same preparation areas, equipment and utensils for preparing cooked and uncooked products.
  • Give examples.

  ....

  ....

c Unhygienic equipment, utensils and preparation methods, e.g. a dirty ladle used for freshly made stock.

....

d Transfer of food poisoning bacteria from the mouth, nose, open cuts and sores and unclean hands to food.
- Give examples.

....

e Incorrect waste disposal, e.g. after straining off a stock pot, leaving the remains lying uncovered for some time before disposing of them into a covered container.
- Give another example.

....

f Incorrect storage of unused items, e.g. unused bones not placed in the correct refrigerator.
- Give another example.

....

g Incorrect storage temperatures, e.g. cooked stock after being cooled not kept in the refrigerator or cold room.
h Incorrect straining procedure, e.g. passing stock through a dirty strainer.
- Give another example.

....

10 Why is it important to keep preparation and cooking areas and equipment hygienic?
  a To prevent contamination of food by food poisoning bacteria, e.g. raw food being prepared on a work surface that was left improperly cleaned from the previous day.
- Give another example.

....

  b To prevent pest infestation and unpleasant odours from arising, e.g. rat droppings soon cause an unpleasant smell.
- Give another example.

....

c To ensure that standards of cleanliness are maintained, e.g. clean hands and knives.
- Give another example.

....

d To comply with the law, e.g. breaking the law can result in heavy fines.
- Give another example.

....

11 Time and temperature are important when cooking stocks.
   a To ensure a correctly cooked stock, e.g. sufficient time is required to extract maximum flavour from the ingredients.
   - Give another example.

....

   b To prevent food poisoning, e.g. if stock is kept in a warm kitchen overnight rather than in a refrigerator it can go sour.
   - Give another example.

....

   c To ensure that loss of nutritional value of prepared food is minimised, e.g. to rapidly chill stock, if it is to be kept, and to avoid keeping stock (if possible, make and use a stock as required).

12 Simmering stock pots for long periods is now considered bad practice. Many establishments do continue to make stocks, as a good stock is often an essential foundation to many culinary dishes. However, it is the policy of some establishments not to make stocks as a matter of hygiene policy.
   - List the stocks you have prepared recently together with any commercial preparations you are either aware of or have used as a substitute.

....

....

....

....

13 Where and from whom can health and safety and food hygiene information be obtained?

....

2ND4.1 *Prepare and cook hot and cold sauces*

Read pages 116–135 of *Practical Cookery*.

1 What are the main contamination threats when preparing, cooking and storing sauces?

....

2 Why are time and temperature important when cooking and storing sauces? State examples.

....

3 Why is it important to keep preparation areas and equipment hygienic?

....

- State examples of any bad practice that you may have observed.

....

4 Sauces.
  a Before commencing work ensure that all preparation and cooking areas and equipment are ready for use and satisfy health, safety and hygiene regulations.
  b Check that work is planned and sufficient time allocated to meet daily schedules.
  c All ingredients used for making sauces must be of the type, quality and quantity required.
  d Ingredients must be correctly prepared and cooked according to the customer, dish and recipe requirements.
  e Sauces must be correctly finished and presented according to customer and dish requirements.
  f After use, all preparation and cooking areas and equipment must be correctly cleaned.

- Name four ways of thickening liquid to form a sauce and give an example for each.

Thickening	Sauce example	Dish for which sauce is suitable
1 roux	béchamel/mornay	poached eggs Florentine
2		
3		
4		

5 When making a sauce the thickening medium should be used in moderation to give a light texture, and not a thick, unpalatable cloying mixture.
   - All sauces should be smooth, but how should they look and taste?

   ....

   - When making a roux-based sauce, a boiling liquid should never be added to a hot roux because the result may be lumpy, and

   ....

   - What are the three degrees to which a roux can be cooked?

Roux	Example of a liquid	Sauce
1		
2		
3 blond	white chicken stock	suprême sauce

   - In addition to butter or margarine, which other ingredient can be used to mix with flour?

   ....

   - What is the benefit of using a slack rather than tight roux when incorporating the liquid?

   ....

   - If a brown roux is overcooked, the starch in the flour will lose some of its thickening property owing to a chemical change known as *dextrinisation*. One effect of this is that the fat will separate from the roux and rise to the surface of the sauce.

- Give two other effects of dextrinisation.

  ....

  ....

- Name four sauces that can be made from béchamel and describe a dish with which each could be served.

Sauce	Dish
1 anchovy	breadcrumbed fried fillets of plaice, anchovy sauce
2	
3	
4 mustard	grilled herring, mustard sauce

- What two additions are made to béchamel for mornay sauce?

  ....

  ....

- How are onions cooked for addition to onion sauce?

  ....

- What are three alternative additions for finishing a cream sauce?

  ....

  ....

  ....

- Why are alternatives to cream sometimes used?

  ....

- Is English mustard always used to make mustard sauce? If not, what is/are the alternative(s)? ....

....

- Name three starches used for thickening sauces.

....

- What are the three stages in thickening a starch-based sauce?

....

....

....

- When finishing a thickened gravy the best starch to use is arrowroot because it gives a completely clear finish to the gravy. As arrowroot is expensive, what substitute can be used?

....

- With what two roast joints is thickened gravy sometimes served?

....

- Is it essential to use a reduction when making a Hollandaise sauce? If not, why not, and what alternative can be used?

....

- How many egg yolks are used to make Hollandaise sauce from 200 g (8 oz) butter:

  1, 2, 3 or 4 egg yolks? ....

- Why is it essential to cook the yolks for an egg-based sauce over a gentle heat and to continually whisk them?

....

- What is the name given to the stage to which yolks are cooked for an egg-based sauce?

  ....

- Why should an egg-based sauce not be served in a hot sauce boat?

  ....

- Give two reasons why an egg-based sauce will curdle.

  ....

- The effect of excess heat will cause the eggs to:

  ....

- What are two ways of reconstituting a curdled sauce?

  ....

  ....

6 In order to reduce the risk of salmonella infection when making egg-based sauces, pasteurised egg yolks may be used. As a further precaution, the warm sauce should then be discarded after it has been kept in a warm kitchen for more than two hours.

  True or false? ....

- Name two fish and two vegetables with which Hollandaise sauce may be served.

  ....

  ....

7 Roasting (page 303, *Practical Cookery*).
- Why is it important to keep the sediment in the tray when making roast gravy?

  ....

- What is this sediment and where does it come from?

  ....

- Why is it important to strain off carefully the fat in the roasting tray after the meat or poultry joint is cooked and removed from the tray?

....

- When roasting a joint of beef, what accompaniment should the strained off beef fat be used for?

....

- What is the reason for carefully browning the sediment in the roasting tray before deglazing with stock?

....

- When roasting poultry, the procedure for making roast gravy is the same as for meat, with the exception of the stock which should be made from the bones and cleaned giblets of the poultry. What are giblets?

....

8 For vegetable gravy, white or brown vegetable sock can be used (page 114, *Practical Cookery*) and lightly thickened with a starch if necessary. If vegetables are cooked in lightly salted water, then the liquid can also be used as a base for vegetable stock.

9 The main contamination threats when preparing, cooking and storing sauces are:
  a The transfer of food poisoning bacteria between cooked sauces and gravies and uncooked raw ingredients kept in the same store, larder or refrigerator, e.g. peeled onions kept in the same store as gravy.
  - Give another example.

....

  b The transfer of food poisoning bacteria by using the same preparation areas, equipment and utensils for preparing cooked and uncooked sauces and gravies, e.g. cutting up vegetables on the same surface which had previously been used for cutting raw meat or poultry and not washed in between.
  - Give another example.

....

  c The transfer of food poisoning bacteria from unhygienic equipment, utensils and preparation methods, e.g. cooking stock in a pan previously used for making a milk-based sauce which had not been properly cleaned.

- Give another example.

....

d The transfer of food poisoning bacteria from the mouth, nose, open cuts and sores and unclean hands to food, e.g. smoking whilst cutting up food, instead of leaving the kitchen for a smoke during a coffee break and then washing the hands before re-commencing work.

e Uncovered food contaminated by pests carrying bacteria.

- Give two examples.

....

f Not disposing of waste or storing unused items in the correct manner, e.g. if sauces or gravies are to be kept overnight, not cooling them or storing in a warm room instead of a refrigerator.

- Give another example.

....

10 What are the quality points to look for in sauce ingredients and finished sauces?

....

....

11 Why is it important to minimise salt added to sauces?

....

12 Which products could be used to substitute high fat ingredients, e.g. butter and cream, when preparing and cooking sauces?

....

2ND4.2 *Prepare and cook soups*

Read pages 135–152 of *Practical Cookery*.

1 Before any preparation, cooking, finishing and serving soups the following points must be borne in mind:

a Preparation and cooking areas and equipment are ready for use and satisfy health, safety and hygiene regulations.

b Work is planned and time allocated to meet daily schedules.

c Ingredients for soups are of the type, quality and quantity required.

d Ingredients are prepared and cooked according to customer and recipe requirements.

e Soups are correctly finished and presented according to customer and dish requirements.

f Preparation, cooking areas and equipment are cleaned after use.

2 Why is it important to keep preparation, cooking and storage areas and equipment hygienic?

....

• List any examples of bad practice that you may have observed.

....

3 What are the main contamination threats when preparing, cooking and storing soups? State examples.

....

....

4 Why are time and temperature important when cooking and storing soups? Give an example.

....

5 Cream soups (page 150, *Practical Cookery*).

• When finishing tomato soup to make it cream of tomato soup, reboil the finished soup, add ½ pint milk and what two other ingredients?

....

• Suggest and name two variations to cream of tomato soup.

....

• When making cream of tomato soup using fresh tomatoes, the colour may be rather pale. How can this be remedied?

....

- When making cream of mushroom soup, which of the following stocks would be used and why: beef, lamb, chicken, or veal?

  ....

- Why is it necessary to remove the bouquet garni before straining a cream soup?

  ....

  ....

- Traditionally, a cream soup is finished with fresh cream. If the fat content of the soup is required to be reduced, natural yoghurt can be used in place of cream. Name two other products which can be used in place of yoghurt.

  ....

- The final consistency of cream soup should be smooth and just of sufficient thickness to lightly coat the back of a spoon. True or false? ....
- Leek and celery are suitable vegetables for use in a cream of vegetable soup. Name three other vegetables.

  ....

- What is an alternative to using all stock for the liquid when making a cream soup?

  ....

- Why is it suitable to use wholemeal flour in place of white flour for cream of vegetable soup, but not for cream of chicken soup?

  ....

6 Broth (page 138, *Practical Cookery*).
  - A broth is a well-flavoured meat or poultry stock cooked together with a good quantity of neatly cut vegetables and garnished with dice of the meat or poultry and a cereal.
    True or false? ....

  - When using a fresh piece of meat for mutton broth, why is it essential to blanch and refresh the meat and set it to cook in a clean pan?

    ....

- What is the approximate cooking time for barley: 15 min., 30 min., 45 min. or 1 hour? ....

- When making mutton broth, why is it not suitable to cook the meat, barley and vegetables together from the start?

  ....

- From the following list of vegetables, select four most suitable for a broth: onions, peas, beans, carrots, cabbage, leeks, turnips, celery.

  ....

- Finally, before serving, a broth is usually finished with chopped ....

- If a boiling fowl is not available to make chicken broth, would 4–6 chicken carcasses be suitable?

  ....

7 Purée soups (pages 149–150, *Practical Cookery*) are made from vegetables, generally with one vegetable dominating, flavoured with herbs and sometimes a little meat, e.g. ham or bacon. They can be made using stock or water, and the thickening agent is solely the vegetables when the soups are made from pulses, e.g. dried peas, beans and lentils. In other cases, if butter, margarine or oil is used to initially sweat the vegetables, then a little flour may be added to absorb the fat. Fried croutons accompany some purée soups, but if fat reduction is required, they may be toasted.

- When making a purée soup using green, yellow split or whole peas, it may be necessary to soak them overnight.

  True or false? ....

- Why may it be necessary to soak pulses overnight?

  ....

- Bouquet garni and knuckle of ham or bacon (optional) are usually added to a pulse soup. Name four other ingredients.

  ....

  ....

- What is the usual accompaniment to purée soups made from pulses?

  ....

- When making lentil soup it is not necessary to soak the lentils overnight. True or

  false? ....

- Select five vegetables suitable for using in a mixed vegetable soup from the
  following: onion, aubergine, tomato, cauliflower, marrow, carrot, mange tout,
  leek, spinach, carrot.

  ....

- What are suitable garnishes for the following purée soups: cauliflower, celery, leek,
  and potato and watercress?

  ....

  ....

- What extra ingredient may be added to purée of lentil and carrot soups to enrich
  the colour? ....

8 What are the quality points to look for in soup ingredients and finished soups?

   ....

9 How would you assess quality in the following soups?

   Cream of cauliflower ....

   Chicken broth ....

   Consommé julienne ....

   Tomato ....

   Lentil ....

   Vegetable ....

   Mushroom ....

10 Why is it important to minimise salt added to soups?

....

11 Which products could be used to substitute high fat ingredients when preparing and cooking soups?

....

Record of Achievement – Completion of Unit 2ND4

Candidate's signature: _____

Assessor's signature: _____

Date: _____

Unit 2ND5

Prepare and cook basic pulse dishes

2ND5.1 *Prepare and cook basic pulse dishes*

Read pages 556–560 of *Practical Cookery*.

Pulses are the dried seeds of plants which form pods, e.g. peas, beans. Pulses are a popular, versatile food which, with a combination of herbs, spices and vegetables can produce many interesting dishes covering almost every course on the menu. Because pulses are good sources of protein and carbohydrate, they help to provide the body with energy and, with the single exception of the soya bean, they are completely deficient in fat. Non-meat eaters find them an important source of protein, and as they also have a high-fibre content this makes them particularly popular with those following a healthy diet.

1 Why is it important to keep preparation, cooking and storage areas and equipment hygienic at all times?

   ....

2 Before starting any work with pulses the following points must be observed:
   a Preparation and cooking areas and equipment are ready for use and satisfy health, safety and hygiene regulations.
   b Work is planned and sufficient time allocated to meet daily schedules.
   c All ingredients used in recipes are of the correct type, quantity and quality.
   d Pulses are correctly prepared according to the recipes.
   e Pulses are correctly combined with other ingredients according to customer and dish requirements.
   f Pulse dishes are cooked, finished and presented according to customer and dish requirements.
   g All preparation and cooking areas and equipment are correctly cleaned after use.

3 Some pulses require pre-soaking before cooking, the soaking time varying considerably according to the type and quality of the pulses and the length of time they have been stored. For soaking, pulses should be comfortably covered in cold water and kept in a cold place. After soaking they should be washed and set to cook in fresh water.
   Red kidney beans *must* always be soaked, washed off and boiled for at least 10 minutes – they contain a substance which unless 'killed' by adequate cooking, can lead to poisoning.

Salt should not be added to pulses before cooking as this will cause the pulse to toughen. Salt should be added as the pulse is almost cooked.
- Name the dishes prepared from pulses that you know.

....

....

....

....

4 List the preparation and cooking methods suitable for different types of pulses. Set out your answer in the form of the chart.

....

....

....

....

....

- If a bowl of dried beans is to be soaked overnight, where is the most suitable place for them to be kept?

....

- Make a list of pulse dishes that can be cooked by the following methods:

stewing or casserole	
grilling or barbecuing	
baking shallow or stir frying	

- Name three dried beans suitable for making into three bean salad and give a reason for your choice.

....

- Name three pulses suitable for making into soup.

  ....

- List the ingredients and method for a burger recipe using a pulse in place of meat.

  ....

  ....

  ....

  ....

  ....

  ....

- Bean goulash is an example of a pulse dish cooked by stewing or in a casserole. Name one other method of stewing beans.

  ....

- Page 499, *Practical Cookery*, shows a recipe for a baked pulse dish. Suggest three ways which the recipe could be varied.

  ....

  ....

  ....

- In the Mexican bean pot recipe on page 502, *Practical Cookery*, what alternatives could you suggest for the following ingredients?

  tomatoes, skinned, de-seeded and diced: ....

  dried marjoram: ....

  chopped chives: ....

5 What products could be used to substitute high fat ingredients when preparing and cooking pulses? Give examples.

  ....

....

....

6 Describe the procedure for storing cooked pulse dishes not required for immediate consumption.

....

7 How can pulses contribute to a healthy balanced diet?

....

8 The main contamination threats when preparing and cooking pulse dishes are:
   a The transfer of food poisoning bacteria by using the same preparation areas, equipment and utensils for both cooked and uncooked products, e.g. using the same spoon for stirring hot pulse cooking and mixing a pulse salad.
   • Give other examples.

....

....

   b The transfer of food poisoning bacteria from unhygienic equipment, utensils and preparation methods, e.g. storing cooked pulses in a container that previously contained meat and that had been wiped out instead of properly washed.
   c The transfer of food poisoning bacteria from the mouth, nose, open cuts and stores and unclean hands to food, e.g. absent-mindedly scratching a sore on the arm and then, without washing the hands, using them to mix a large quantity of pulse salad.
   • Give another example.

....

   d Uncovered food contaminated by pests carrying bacteria.
   • Give an example from your experience.

....

   e Incorrect disposal for waste or storing unused items, e.g. leaving a bowl of cooked pulse uncovered in a warm room overnight.
   • Give another example.

....

f Contamination from unclean pulses. Pulses should always be carefully picked over to look for any foreign bodies before being used, e.g. one or two unsound beans could be sufficient to contaminate a large quantity.

9 Preparation and cooking areas and equipment must be kept hygienic at all times.

10 Time and temperature are important when cooking pulse dishes, otherwise the pulse recipe will be improperly cooked. They are also important to prevent food poisoning, and to ensure that any loss of nutritional value of prepared food is minimised.
   • Give other examples.

   ....

Record of Achievement – Completion of Unit 2ND5

Candidate's signature: _____

Assessor's signature: _____

Date: _____

Unit 2ND6

Prepare and cook basic rice dishes

2ND6.1 *Prepare and cook basic rice dishes*

Read pages 235–239 of *Practical Cookery*.

1 It is important to always ensure that:
   a Preparation areas and equipment are ready for use and satisfy health, safety and food hygiene regulations.
   b Rice is of the type, quality and quantity required.
   c Ingredients are prepared and cooked according to dish requirements.
   d Prepared rice dishes are finished and presented according to customer and dish requirements.
   e Finished rice dishes not for immediate consumption are stored in accordance with laid-down procedures.
   f Preparation and cooking areas and equipment are correctly cleaned after use.

2 What are the main contamination threats when preparing and storing rice?

   ....

3 Why are time and temperature important when cooking rice and keeping cooked rice hot?

   ....

4 Why is it important to keep preparation and storage areas and equipment hygienic?
   • List any examples of bad practice that you may have observed.

   ....

   ....

5 How can the fibre content of rice dishes be increased? Give examples.

   ....

   ....

6 What preparation/cooking methods are suitable for different types of rice dishes? Give examples and set your answer out in the form of a graph.

....

....

....

....

....

7 Which products can be used as substitutes for high fat ingredients when preparing and cooking rice dishes? Give examples of three dishes.

....

....

....

8 The versatility of rice can be illustrated by its use in the recipes in *Practical Cookery* on pages: 181, 210, 236–8, 271, 340, 371, 408, 459, 464, 505, 618, 633.
Rice is the principal food crop for about half of the world's population. In order to grow, rice requires more water than any other cereal crop. There are around 250 different varieties of rice. Indian rice is long grained and tends to be dry, flaky and easily separated when cooked; Japanese is short grained, and moist, firm and sticky when cooked. Japanese rice contains more waxy starch.

9 Why is long grain rice best suited for savoury dishes and plain boiled rice?

....

• Give two examples of long grained rice.

....

Carolina type (American) rice is sometimes known as all-purpose rice as it can be used for savoury or sweet dishes.
• Why is short grain rice best suited for milk puddings and sweet dishes?

....

Arborio is one of the best-known types of short grain rice and comes from Italy.
- What is brown rice and why is it more nutritious?

....

- What is wild rice?

....

- Ground rice is used for milk puddings. Name two other products made from processed rice and give an example of the use of each.

....

....

- Why is it important to pick and wash rice, and why use plenty of boiling water for cooking (page 235, *Practical Cookery*)?

....

- What type of dishes should always be accompanied by plain boiled or steamed rice?

....

- Why is it important to measure the amount of stock to the amount of rice when cooking a pilau (pages 236–237, *Practical Cookery*).

....

- Too much stock will make the pilau ....

- Too little stock will make the pilau ....
- In a hot oven, pilau rice should cook in approximately 5 min., 10 min., 15 min.,

  20 min. or 25 min.? ....
- Why must a pilau be removed from the pan immediately it is cooked?

....

- When finally mixing in butter to a pilau, why is a two-pronged fork ideal?

....

- Why is short grain rice not suitable for pilau?

  ....

- Wild rice may also be braised or cooked pilau. True or false? ....
  (pages 237–238, *Practical Cookery*, show variations on a pilau, other additions can include saffron, pre-soaked raisins or sultanas.)
- Give a suggestion of your own idea of an interesting dish of rice pilau.

  ....

  ....

The difference between a pilau and a risotto is that in a pilau the rice grains when cooked should be dryish and separate easily, in a risotto the end product is moist.
- What is the main difference in the cooking technique for a pilau and risotto?

  ....

- As risotto is an Italian dish, a short grain or ....

  rice is used. True or false? ....
- What is the finish to a risotto?

  ....

As with pilau, there are many variations that can be made to a basic risotto. A popular one is fish (usually shellfish) when a fish stock is used for cooking the rice.

Basmati rice is grown in the foothills of the Himalayas. This narrow long rain rice is one of the finest types of rice. Basmati should be soaked before cooking to remove the excess starch.
- List two dishes which Basmati rice could accompany.

  ....

- Steamed rice is the traditional method for preparing rice for Chinese dishes. Certain types of rice are not suitable for steaming. These are:

  ....

- For steaming rice in a pan see page 236 of *Practical Cookery*. Rice can also be steamed in a steamer: wash the rice, and drain and dry using absorbent paper. Place the rice in a bowl and add 175 ml (.................. fl oz) of water to approx. 225 g (.................. oz) of rice.

- Place the bowl in a rice steamer and cook over boiling water until tender.
- Once cooked, the rice should be allowed to stand in the covered steamer for 10 minutes. Why is this necessary?

....

- Fried rice is cooked rice which is stir fried with other ingredients and usually finished with soy sauce. There are many different recipes and variations. List at least four different garnishes for fried rice.

....

....

Record of Achievement – Completion of Unit 2ND6

Candidate's signature: _____

Assessor's signature: _____

Date: _____

Unit 2ND7

Prepare and cook basic dough products

2ND7.1 *Prepare basic dough products for cooking*

Read pages 638–650 of *Practical Cookery*.

1 Dough is kneaded, moistened flour. Before commencing any dough preparation the following points must be observed:
   a Preparation areas and equipment are ready for use and satisfy health, safety and hygiene regulations.
   b Work is planned and time appropriately allocated to meet daily schedules.
   c Dough ingredients (flour, yeast, etc.) are of the type, quality and quantity required.
   d Dough is prepared according to product requirements.
   e Prepared dough is stored in accordance with food hygiene regulations.
   f Preparation areas and equipment are correctly cleaned after use.

2 Why is wheatmeal/wholemeal flour considered to be healthier than white flour?

   ....

3 Yeast.
   • Complete the following six quality and storage points for fresh yeast:

   Yeast should be wrapped and stored in ....

   It should be ordered only ....

   It must be perfectly .... and ....

   The smell must be ....

   Yeast should .... easily.

   The colour of yeast is ....
   (Yeast is also available as a dried product, which if kept in sealed containers has a much longer life than fresh yeast.)
   • As dried yeast has been dehydrated, what has to be done with it to make it ready for use?

   ....

120

- Complete the following seven important points to remember when using yeast:

  Yeast should be removed from the refrigerator and used at .... temperature.
  What is the effect of salt on the working of yeast? ....

  The more salt used, the .... the action of the yeast.

  The best temperature for yeast action is ....

  The best temperature for liquid for mixing dough is ....

  Temperatures over .... can destroy yeast and make any subsequent dough unusable.

  Yeast can sustain .... temperatures without damage.

- What do you understand by the terms kneading and proving?

  ....

  ....

- What is meant by overproving?

  ....

- What are the causes of overproving?

  ....

4 Yeast dough (page 639, *Practical Cookery*).
   - Why is the flour warmed before making a yeast dough?

     ....

   - What is the first stage in using yeast before adding to the flour?

     ....

   - When the yeast mixture is added to the flour and sprinkled with a little flour, the bowl is covered with a cloth and left in a warm place. What process takes

     place next? ....

- Complete the following to test your underpinning knowledge.
  When the remainder of the ingredients for the dough are added the kneading process takes place, which means initially mixing, then working the dough firmly

  with both hands on a lightly floured surface until .... and free from

  .... ? Pushing the dough out into a thick strip and folding it can be part of this process. After the dough has been kneaded, it is returned to the basin, covered with a cloth and left in a warm place until it has doubled in size. This is

  known as .... ?

- After the dough has .... it is then knocked back, which means expelling all the air by firm use of both hands.

  The dough is now ready to be moulded into the desired shape(s) and sizes. Bread rolls can be shaped in a variety of ways (page 644, *Practical Cookery*). The dough is initially divided into even-sized pieces to ensure the rolls are of the same size.

  Plaiting: the piece of dough is shaped into three equal thick lengths which are then laid side by side; start interlacing from the centre working out to each end.

  After the dough has been moulded into the desired shape, it is either placed on a greased baking sheet (rolls) or into greased bread tins (loaves) covered with a cloth and left to double in size. Finally, the dough products may be carefully brushed with egg wash and are ready for the oven.

- What is egg wash? ....

- What is its purpose? ....

- What is this process called? ....
- What would happen if you brushed the proven dough too firmly?

  ....

- To make a wholemeal or wheatmeal dough, what is used in place of white flour?

  ....

- To make basic bun dough, three extra ingredients are added to flour, milk and water and yeast. What are these?

  ....

- Are these extra ingredients added to the bun dough before or after the yeast has fermented? ....

- What are the signs that show the yeast has fermented?

....

5 The main contamination threats when preparing and cooking dough products are:
   a The transfer of food poisoning bacteria by using the same preparation areas, equipment and utensils for preparing cooked and uncooked products.
   - Give an example.

   ....

   b The transfer of food poisoning bacteria from unhygienic equipment, utensils and preparation methods.
   - Give an example.

   ....

   c The transfer of food poisoning bacteria from the mouth, nose, open cuts and sores and unclean hands to food.
   - Give an example.

   ....

   d Uncovered food contaminated by pests carrying bacteria.
   - Give an example.

   ....

   e Not disposing of waste or storing unused items in the correct manner.

   ....

   - Give an example.

6 Keeping preparation and cooking areas and equipment hygienic.
   a To prevent contamination of food by food poisoning bacteria.
   - Give an example.

   ....

b To prevent pest infestation and unpleasant smells.
• Give an example.

....

c To ensure standards of cleanliness are maintained.
• Give an example.

....

d To comply with the law.
• Give an example.

....

7 Time and temperature are vitally important in the preparation of dough products.
• Give two reasons why.

....

....

As yeast is a form of plant life (fungus) consisting of minute cells, these cells grow and multiply at blood heat provided they are fed with sugar and liquid. The sugar causes the fermentation which is the production of gas (carbon dioxide) and alcohol in the form of small bubbles in the dough. When warmth is applied, the dough rises. The timing of this process has to be co-ordinated with temperature.
• Without correct application of time and temperature, the dough products will not be .... for the cooking process.

8 List the advantages of using:

a dried yeast

....

....

....

b fresh yeast

....

....

....

9 Briefly describe the following preparation methods:

mixing ....

kneading ....

proving ....

folding ....

glazing ....

shaping ....

rolling ....

portioning ....

10 Describe the following quality points associated with a basic dough mix.

a texture ....

b aroma ....

11 How can the fibre content of dough products be increased?

....

2ND7.2 *Cook basic dough products*

1 Basic rules for cooking any dough products:

a Cooking areas and equipment must be ready for use and satisfy health, safety and hygiene regulations.

b Work is planned and time appropriately allocated to meet daily schedules.

c Dough is suitably prepared for the cooking process.

d Dough is cooked according to product requirements.

e Cooked dough products are finished according to product requirements.

f Finished dough products are stored in accordance with food hygiene regulations.

g Preparation and cooking areas are correctly cleaned after use.

2 Name six different types of dough products you are familiar with.

....

....

3 Bread loaves can be made in many shapes and sizes, and either cooked in bread tin moulds or free standing on baking sheets, to test when the bread loaves are cooked, turn them upside down and tap their bottoms sharply with the knuckles. The loaves should sound hollow to indicate that they have lost much of their moisture during baking. (For bread rolls, see page 642, *Practical Cookery.*)

• Why is the flour and liquid used warm when making bread dough?

....

- Why is it necessary for the yeast to ferment before mixing it into the dough?

  ....

- When kneading bread dough, what is the sign that indicates it has been sufficiently kneaded?

  ....

- When a dough is sufficiently proved, how large should it be?

  ....

- What will be the effect of extreme heat on the yeast at any stage of bread making and what will be the subsequent effect on the bread?

  ....

4   Recipes for bun dough, bun wash, fruit, hot-cross buns, Bath, Chelsea, Swiss buns and doughnuts can be found on pages 643–645, *Practical Cookery*.
- The purpose of using bun wash on certain buns is to give them a glaze or shine. What are the ingredients in a bun wash and when should it be brushed on the buns?

  ....

- Swiss buns when cooked are not finished with bun wash, they are finished (iced) with what?

  ....

(Fruit buns are glazed with bun wash as soon as they are cooked, Swiss buns are left to cool before icing.)
- How many buns are obtained from a 200 g (½ lb) flour bun dough mix 4, 6, 8, 10 or 12? ....

5   Name two dough products which may be deep fried.

  ....

- What is the frying temperature for doughnuts: 125°C, 150°C, 175°C or 200°C?

  ....

6   Hygiene (pages 639–41, *Practical Cookery*).
   •   There are five main contamination threats when preparing and cooking dough products. Name them and give examples.

   ....

   ....

   ....

   ....

   ....

   •   It is important to keep preparation, cooking and storage areas and equipment hygienic for four good reasons. Name them.

   ....

   ....

   ....

   ....

7   Time and temperature are particularly important when cooking dough products, otherwise a correctly cooked product will not result.
   •   Give another reason.

   ....

Record of Achievement – Completion of Unit 2ND7

Candidate's signature: _____

Assessor's signature: _____

Date: _____

Prepare and cook basic pastry dishes

2ND8.1 *Prepare fresh pastry*

Read pages 650–692 of *Practical Cookery*.

1 Always comply with the following points:
   a Preparation areas and equipment are ready for use and satisfy health, safety and hygiene regulations.
   b Work is planned and time appropriately allocated to meet daily schedules.
   c Pastry ingredients are of the type, quality and quantity required, e.g. correct types of flour, fats with no signs of rancidity, and fresh untainted eggs.
   d Pastry is prepared according to dish requirements.
   e Prepared pastry is stored in accordance with food hygiene regulations.
   f Preparation areas and equipment are correctly cleaned after use.

2 Pastry (pages 661–667, *Practical Cookery*).
   • What is the proportion of flour to fat for short pastry: 1–1, 1½–1, 2–1, 2½–1 or 3–1?

   ....

   • Why is it important to sieve flour and salt before making pastry?

   ....

   • Why is it an advantage to have cool hands when mixing short pastry?

   ....

   • What is the flour content for wholemeal short pastry?

   ....

3 Describe how you would produce large quantities of short pastry.

   ....

   ....

   ....

- Give three uses for short pastry.

  ....

4 Give two reasons for each of the following faults in short pastry:

hard: ....

soft, crumbly: ....

blistered: ....

soggy: ....

shrunken: ....

- What type of flour is used in making short and sweet pastry? ....
- What is the proportion of flour to fat when making sweet pastry:
  1–1, 2–1, 3–1, 4–1, 4–2, or 4–2½? ....
- What are the two ingredients added to sweet pastry not used in short pastry?

  ....

- There are two methods of making sweet pastry, one is the creaming method, the other is ....
- Why is it necessary to rest sweet pastry before rolling?

  ....

- Where is the best place to rest sweet pastry?

  ....

- What is the flour difference when making wholemeal sweet pastry?

  ....

- Sweet pastry is also known as sugar pastry. True or false? ....
- Name three items made from sweet pastry.

  ....

  ....

- What type of flour is used in making puff pastry? Why?

  ....

- What is the ratio of flour to fat for making puff pastry: 1–1, 1½–1, 2–1, 2½–1, 3–2 or

  5–2? ....

- The reason for adding a little acid to puff pastry is to strengthen the gluten which helps to make a stronger dough. Any one of three acids may be added: ascorbic

  acid, tartaric acid, and .... acid.
- Why is it important to make a strong dough for puff pastry?

  ....

- When placing the fat on the basic dough, it is important to ensure that the texture of the butter is the same as that of the dough. True or false? ....
- What would happen if a hard fat were folded into a soft dough?

  ....

- Describe one double turn of puff pastry. What must be done before making a further turn?

  ....

- Why is it necessary to rest puff pastry in a cool place between turns?

  ....

Where and when time permits, puff pastry can also be given single rather than double turns. In this case, six single turns are given, two at a time with a 2–3 hour rest in a cool place in between each pair of turns. Ask your tutor or trainer to show you a single turn.
- Why is it essential to keep the ends and sides square when rolling out puff pastry for turning?

  ....

- Well-made puff pastry when baked should have a light flaky formation. What causes this flakiness?

  ....

- Cream horns and jam turnovers can be made from puff pastry. Name four other items.

  ....

  ....

- Give two reasons for each of the following faults in puff pastry:

  not flaky: ....

  fat oozes out: ....

  hard: ....

  shrunken: ....

  soggy: ....

  uneven rise: ....
- Puff pastry should be wrapped in a cloth or plastic and kept in a refrigerator in between turns and when it is ready for use. True or false? ....
- What is the difference in the flour to fat ratio between puff and rough puff pastry?

  ....

- What is the method of adding fat to flour when making rough puff pastry: rubbing in finely, creaming, rubbing in pieces, or folding in? ....
- Can wholemeal flour be used in making puff and rough puff pastry and, if so, in what proportion? ....
- What type of flour is used in making suet pastry?

  ....

- What is the raising agent used in suet pastry?

  ....

- What is the ratio of flour to fat for suet pastry: 1–1, 1½–1, 2–1, 2½–1 or 3–1? ....
- Sufficient water should be used in making suet pastry to form a soft dough, firm

  dough or fairly stiff dough? ....
- Give a reason for the following faults in suet pastry:

  heavy and soggy: ....

tough: ....
- Name three dishes using suet pastry.

....

....

5   How should the following pastry not for immediate consumption be stored?
short pastry ....
sweet pastry ....
suet pastry ....
puff pastry ....
choux pastry ....

6   The main contamination threats when preparing and storing fresh pastry are:
   a   The transfer of food poisoning bacteria by using the same preparation areas, equipment and utensils for preparing cooked and uncooked products, e.g. using a bowl in which eggs were beaten for storing pastry without properly cleaning and drying the bowl.
   - Give another example.

....

   b   The transfer of food poisoning bacteria from unhygienic equipment, utensils and preparation methods, e.g. sifting flour through a dirty sieve (the flour sieve should be kept in a clean drawer).
   - Give another example.

....

   c   The transfer of food poisoning bacteria from the mouth, nose, open cuts and sores and unclean hands to food, e.g. failing to wash the hands after going to the toilet and then rubbing pastry.
   - Give another example.

....

   d   Uncovered food contaminated by pests carrying bacteria, e.g. an uncovered flour bin can attract many hungry pests.
   - Give another example.

....

e Not disposing of waste or storing unused items in the correct manner, e.g. left over pastry left unwrapped and out of the refrigerator.
  • Give another example.

....

7 Time and temperature are important when preparing fresh pastry because unless pastry is made quickly, particularly in a warm kitchen, it will become too soft and difficult to handle.
  • Give another example.

....

8 Name four items produced from choux pastry.

....

....

9 If basic choux pastry is overcooked the result will be greasy and ....
  • If the choux pastry mixture is soft and does not aerate this may be due to:
    flour insufficiently cooked

....

    oven too cool

....

10 Describe the texture, appearance and consistency of the following freshly prepared pastries:
   Short pastry ....

   Choux pastry ....

   Rough puff pastry ....

11 Describe the following processing methods:

   cutting ....

   rolling ....

   shaping ....

   lining ....

2ND8.2 *Cook basic pastry dishes*

1 Before starting work ensure that:
   a Preparation and cooking areas and equipment are ready for use and satisfy health, safety and hygiene regulations.
   b Work is planned and time appropriately allocated to meet daily schedules, e.g. unless sufficient time is allowed, tasks will not be carried out properly and results will be poor.
   c Pastry dishes are of the type, quality and quantity required.
   d Pastry is suitably prepared according to dish requirements.
   e Pastry is correctly combined with other ingredients according to customer and recipe requirements.
   f Pastry dishes are cooked according to customer and dish requirements.
   g Pastry dishes for immediate consumption are finished and presented according to customer and dish requirements.
   h Pastry dishes not for immediate consumption are stored in accordance with the food hygiene regulations.
   i Preparation and cooking areas and equipment are correctly cleaned after use.

2 Short pastry.
   • Name three fruits suitable for fruit pies.

   ....

   • Name three pairs of fruit suitable for fruit pies.

   ....

   ....

   • All fruit for fruit pies should be washed. True or false? ....
   • Name two spices that can be used to flavour an apple pie.

   ....

   • When rolling out pastry for a fruit pie, is it important not to stretch it because if the pastry is stretched when rolled or laid out, when the pie is placed in a hot oven the pastry will ....
   • What is the purpose of brushing a fruit pie with milk and sprinkling with castor sugar before baking?

   ....

   • At what temperature should a fruit pie be placed in the oven: 180°C, 200°C, 220°C, 240°C or 260°C? ....

- Name three suitable accompaniments for a fruit pie.

  ....

3 Sweet pastry.
   - After making sweet pastry and before using, it should be allowed to rest in the refrigerator before rolling it out. This allows the pastry to relax and lessens the risk of it .... when cooking, and allows the pastry to firm up and make it easier to ....
   - If the bottom of the flan or tartlet cases are not pricked with a fork while uncooked, what is likely to happen when they are cooking?

   ....

   - What is the oven temperature required for baking a fresh fruit flan: 150–180°C, 200–230°C or 250–280°C? ....
   - When should the flan ring be removed from a flan case and how can a shine be given to the sides?

   ....

   - Why is a flan case lined and filled with baking beans when cooking blind?

   ....

   - What is the difference between a fruit tartlet and a fruit barquet?

   ....

   - When finishing a banana flan, why is it important to cover the sliced bananas with apricot glaze or flan glaze as quickly as possible?

   ....

4 Puff or rough puff pastry.
   - When making cream horns after the pastry has been cut into strips, why is it important to moisten each strip on one side?

   ....

   - When making cream horns, at which end of the moulds is the pastry strip first started?

   ....

- When many puff pastry goods are almost cooked they can be given an appetising, shiny finish by sprinkling with icing sugar and returning briefly to a hot oven. This has the effect of lightly caramelising the sugar, making it shine. What is this process called?

  ....

- After cream horns are baked and cooled, how are they finished before serving?

  ....

5 List the advantages of using frozen prepared puff pastry.

  ....

  ....

  ....

  ....

- Unless a good quality, carefully prepared and handled puff pastry is used for making puff pastry cases, then the cases will not be suitable for being filled. Why?

  ....

- Small puff pastry cases are known as ....
- Large puff pastry cases are known as ....
- After puff pastry cases are baked and cooled, what should be done to make them ready for use? ....

  ....

- Suggest two uses each for serving cold bouchées as pastries and two for serving hot as savouries?

  ....

  ....

- What thickness should puff or rough puff pastry be rolled for making sausage rolls: 2 mm (1/16 in), 4 mm (1/8 in), 6 mm (1/4 in), or 1.2 cm (1/2 in)? ....
- Mince pies can be made with puff or rough puff pastry, or they can also be made using two other types of pastry. What are they?

  ....

6 Suet pastry.
- Name two suitable fillings for a fruit steamed suet pudding.

  ....

- Why is it essential to tightly cover a suet pudding to be steamed with either greased greaseproof paper, silicone paper, a pudding cloth or foil?

  ....

- Why should puddings only be placed in the steamer when the pressure gauge indicates that the required degree of temperature has been reached?

  ....

- What is meant in relation to steamed suet puddings by:

  moulding: ....

  traying-up: ....

  loading: ....
- Describe the making of a steamed jam roll.

  ....

  ....

  ....

  ....

  ....

- Name four dried fruits suitable for use in a steamed suet pudding.

  ....

- Name two sauces suitable for serving with a steamed golden syrup suet pudding.

  ....

- Name two variations for a steamed steak pudding.

  ....

- In addition to the meat content, what other seasonings may be added to a steamed pudding?

  ....

- What is the appropriate cooking time for a four portion meat pudding using raw meat: 1½ hrs, 2½ hrs, 3½ hrs, 4½ hrs or 5½ hrs? ....
- How many dumplings can be made out of 100 g (4 oz) suet paste: 2, 4, 6, 8, 10, 12, 14 or 16? ....
- When and how are dumplings cooked in a dish of braised steak and dumplings?

  ....

7 The main contamination threats when preparing, storing and cooking pastry dishes are:
   a The transfer of food poisoning bacteria by using the same preparation areas, equipment and utensils for preparing cooked and uncooked products, e.g. using same area for making sausage rolls and finished fresh cream cakes.
   b The transfer of food poisoning bacteria from unhygienic equipment, utensils and preparation methods, e.g. beating eggs in an unclean bowl using a dirty whisk.
   c The transfer of food poisoning bacteria from the mouth, nose, open cuts, and sores and unclean hands to food, e.g. rubbing in fat to flour using unwashed hands with long, dirty finger nails.
   d Uncovered food contaminated by pests carrying bacteria, e.g. small insects can easily get into flour if it is left uncovered.
   e Not disposing of waste or storing unused items in the correct manner, e.g. storing cream-filled pastries on an unprotected shelf without refrigeration.

8 It is important to keep preparation areas and equipment hygienic in order to:
   a Prevent contamination of food by food poisoning bacteria.
   • Give an example.

   ....

   b Prevent pest infestation and unpleasant smells from arising, e.g. pests are particularly attracted to foods in the pastry areas because of their sweetness.
   c Ensure that standards of cleanliness are maintained, e.g. many items used in pastry work (whisks, mixing machines, etc.) are likely harbours for bacteria.
   d Comply with the law, e.g. failure to comply with the law can lead to a conviction and a subsequent heavy fine.

9 Time and temperature are important when cooking pastry:
   a To ensure correctly cooked pastry dishes.
   • Give an example.

   ....

b To ensure that loss of nutritional value of prepared food is minimised.
• Give an example.

....

• List the pastry items you have recently prepared from the following:
a Short pastry:

....

....

....

....

....

b Sweet pastry:

....

....

....

....

....

c Puff pastry:

....

....

....

....

....

10 Name the hygiene precautions taken by the pastry department you have recently worked in, e.g. all risk items stored at 3°C refrigerated separately.

....

....

....

....

....

....

....

....

11 List basic convenience pastry mixes with which you are familiar.

....

....

12 Name three products prepared from the following pastries.

Pastry	Products
Short	
Sweet	
Suet	
Choux	
Frozen puff	
Convenience short pastry mix	

13 Describe the quality points for assessing the following pastry products.

Product	Texture	Aroma	Appearance	Flavour
Fresh apple pie	Short pastry, soft fruit	Freshly baked pastry, fresh apples	Golden brown, sugar top	Rich flavour of apples not too sweet short pastry
Chocolate eclairs				
Apricot flan				
Steamed suet sultana roll				
Mille feuille				
Apple turnovers				
Mincemeat jalousie				
Almond pithivier				

14 Name two pastry products which may be produced from the following finishing methods.

Finishing method	Product
Dusting	Apple pie – dusted with castor sugar
Filling	Mille-feuille with fresh or pastry cream and jam
Piping	Cream horns with jam and cream

....

....

15 Time and temperature is extremely important when storing, preparing and cooking pastry. Why?

....

....

Record of Achievement – Completion of Unit 2ND8

Candidate's signature: _____

Assessor's signature: _____

Date: _____

Unit 2ND9

Prepare, cook and finish basic cakes, sponges and scones

2ND9.1 *Prepare basic cakes, sponges and scones*

Read pages 693–720 of *Practical Cookery*.

1 Before starting work it is important that:
   a Preparation areas and equipment are ready for use and satisfy health, safety and hygiene regulations.
   b Work is planned and time allocated to meet daily schedules.
   c Ingredients are of the type, quality and quantity required.
   d Mixtures are prepared according to product requirements.
   e Prepared mixtures are stored in accordance with food hygiene regulations.
   f Preparation areas and equipment are correctly cleaned after use.

2 If you find any problems with the quality of ingredients who should you report this to?

   ....

3 The following are methods of preparation which relate to the quality of the end product.

   Whisking
   Folding
   Greasing
   Glazing
   Portioning

   Describe three of the above preparation methods.

   ....

   ....

   ....

   ....

....

....

....

....

....

4 Cakes.
- Complete the following requirements for making light scones:
    1 The correct proportion of .... to flour.
    2 After rubbing-in fat to flour, when adding liquid mix to ....
    3 The comparatively small amount of ....
    4 Quick and .... handling.
- Cake mixtures containing baking powder should be baked as soon as they are mixed. True or false? ....
- The effect of over-use of baking powder in cakes is that they will have a .... taste, and they will .... in the middle.
- The effect of under-use of baking powder is that the cake texture will be ....

    Therefore, baking powder must always be carefully and accurately measured before being used.
- What adjustments are required to the basic scone mix to make wholemeal scones and fruit scones?

....

- Describe each method for making a basic small cake mixture.
    1 Rubbing in:

....

....

....

....

    2 Creaming:

....

....

....

....

- What is the difference in technique when adding the beaten eggs to each method?
  1 Rubbing:

....

....

  2 Creaming:

....

....

- Irrespective of which method used, what is the correct consistency for the mixture?

....

- What is the alternative to using flour and baking powder?

....

- What type of flour is used for small cakes? ....
- There are six possible reasons for faults in cakes. Give one more reason for each fault.

1 Uneven texture: (a) fat insufficiently rubbed in
                             (b) too little liquid
                             (c) ....

2 Close texture: (a) hands too hot when rubbing in
                             (b) too much fat
                             (c) ....

3 Dry: (a) oven too hot
                             (b) ....

4 Bad shape: (a) too much liquid
                             (b) too much baking powder
                             (c) ....

5 Fruit sunk: (a) fruit wet

                        (b) too much liquid
6 Cracked: (a) too much baking powder
                        (b) ....

- Queen cakes are made from the basic small cake mixture with the addition of 4 oz (100 g) washed and dried mixed fruit. True or false? ....
- What fruit would be used in Queen cakes?

....

- When making a large fruit cake, the fat and sugar are: creamed until soft and ....; and the beaten eggs are added .... and in between.
- What is the advantage of using silicone over greaseproof paper for lining cake tins?

....

5   Sponges.
- There are five possible reasons for faults in sponges. Give another reason in each case:

1 Close texture: (a) underbeating
                          (b) oven too cool or too hot
                          (c) ....
2 Holey texture: (a) flour insufficiently folded in
                          (b) ....
3 Cracked crust: (a) ....
4 Sunken: (a) tin removed during baking
                          (b) ....
5 White spots on surface: ....
- Give the proportion of ingredients for a Victoria sponge sandwich.

Butter or margarine: ....   Flour: ....
Castor sugar: ....   Eggs: ....
- What type of flour is used for a Victoria sponge? ....
- What is the basic difference between making a Victoria sponge and a Genoese sponge?

....

- The basic principle of making a Genoese sponge is to form the lightest, aerated mixture of eggs and sugar. Why then is it essential that both the flour and melted butter be added as carefully and gently as possible?

....

- Give one other reason for faults in Genoese sponges.

1 Close texture: (a) too much flour
               (b) eggs and sugar over or under-beaten
               (c) ....

2 Sunken: (a) too much sugar
               (b) oven too hot
               (c) ....

3 Heavy: (a) butter too hot
               (b) butter insufficiently mixed in
               (c) ....

- What is the name given to the beaten eggs and sugar when they have reached the final stage and are ready for the flour to be folded in?

....

- What is the method of preparing a mould for a Genoese sponge?

....

- What variation is required from the basic recipe to make a chocolate Genoese sponge?

....

....

- What type of flour is used for Genoese sponge?

....

- The basic method of making a sponge for a Swiss roll is the same as for Genoese sponge. True or false? ....

6 Why is portioning so important?

....

7 A simple shortbread biscuit recipe is (add the ingredients in each case):
150 g (6 oz) ....   50 g (2 oz) ....
100 g (4 oz) ....   pinch of salt ....

- When the shortbread biscuit mix is shaped and placed on a lightly greased baking sheet, it is pricked with a fork and marked with a knife into the required size and shapes. Why is it important to do this before baking?

....

147

8   Describe the quality points of the following products.

Product	Texture	Appearance	Consistency
Basic convenience sponge mixture			
Freshly baked scones			
Fresh raw genoise sponge mixture			Ribbon stage
Madeira cake mixture (batter method)			
Baked rich fruit cake		Dark golden colour, good visual fruit appearance	

9   What special safety precautions must you observe when preparing and baking cakes, sponges and scones?

   ....

10   What are the main contamination threats that have to be considered when preparing and storing basic cake, sponge and scone mixtures?

   ....

11   Time and temperature are extremely important when preparing cakes, sponges and scones, both when baking, preparing and storing. State the reasons why.
   1 in baking ....
   2 in preparing ....
   3 in storage ....

12   Name the preparation methods for the following products:
   Scones ....
   Chocolate genoise ....
   Swiss roll ....
   Battenburg ....
   Sponge fingers ....
   Shortbread biscuits ....

13 How can the high fat content of cakes and scones be reduced?

....

14 Name the different types of fats which are used in baking. State which contain polyunsaturates.

....

15 In order to produce a product with a higher fibre content, a percentage of the white flour content may be substituted with wholemeal flour. Often the recipe has to be modified in order to achieve a product of the desired quality. Write down a recipe for a cake, sponge or scone of your choice, where some of the white flour has been substituted with wholemeal.

....

....

....

....

....

16 The amount of sugar in pastry products can also contribute to healthy catering practices. List a range of products where the sugar may be reduced without impairing the quality of the product.

....

....

....

....

2ND9.2 *Cook and finish basic cakes, sponges and scones*

1 When cooking cakes, sponges and scones the following points are important:
   a Preparation and cooking areas and equipment are ready for use and satisfy health, safety and hygiene regulations.
   b Work is planned and time appropriately allocated to meet daily schedules.

    c Cake, sponge and scone mixtures are of the type, quality and quantity required.
    d Mixtures are suitably prepared for the cooking process.
    e Cakes, sponges and scones are cooked according to product requirements.
    f Cakes, sponges and scones are finished in accordance with product requirements.
    g Finished products are stored in accordance with food hygiene regulations.
    h Preparation and cooking areas are correctly cleaned after use.

2   Baking (pages 89–91, *Practical Cookery*).
- The following key words are frequently used during the baking of cakes, sponges and scones. Give an example of the use of each one.
  Greasing: ....
  Marking: (a) marking shortbread biscuits with a sharp-bladed knife prior to baking.
             (b) ....
  Loading means the economic use of oven space to ensure the maximum amount of food is organised to be baked, thus minimising .... and loss of
  ....
  Brushing: (a) egg wash on sausage rolls to improve colour and appearance
             (b) ....
  Cooling is the placing of freshly baked goods on wire grids or .... so that air circulates around the goods and prevents the bases becoming ....
  Finishing (the final finish applied to certain baked goods).
  Recovery time is the time required for the oven .... to reach the
  .... before cooking further batches of goods.
  Dusting: (a) sprinkling with flour.
             (b) ....
  Glazing usually refers to the final sprinkling of certain puff pastry goods with icing sugar and returning to a hot oven for a few seconds. This causes the surface to
  .... and ....

3   Cakes, sponges and scones.
- What is the oven temperature for baking scones: 100°C, 150°C, 200°C, 250°C or 300°C? ....
- When testing a large fruit cake to see if it is cooked, where should the thin needle be placed and what should be the appearance of the needle when withdrawn?

....

....

- When baking cakes, sponges and scones, why is it important to open and close the door gently?

....

- If cakes, sponges or scones are moved or shaken before they are set, e.g. when half cooked, what will be the likely effect?

....

4   Hygiene (see pages 43–56, *Practical Cookery*).

5   Time and temperature are important when cooking cakes and biscuits otherwise finished goods will be either undercooked, overcooked, too pale, overcoloured or unattractive in appearance, and therefore a waste of ingredients (money), time (money), and oven heat (money).

6   How should cakes, sponges and scones not for immediate consumption be stored?

....

7   The following terms relate to processes used in the production of cakes, sponges and scones. Explain each term.
Shaping ....

Spreading ....

Filling ....

Rolling ....

Lining ....

8   Give an example of a product produced from:
Shaping ....
Filling ....
Rolling ....

9   Give an example of a cake, sponge and scone produced from the following finishing methods:

Finishing method	Product
Turning out	Rich fruit cake
Spreading	....
Cooling	....
Glazing	....

Trimming ....

Basic piping ....

Sprinkling ....

Dusting   Swiss roll

Dredging ....

Rolling ....

Filling ....

It is important to observe safe working practices at all times, especially when using dangerous equipment and hot ovens.

10 Why is it essential that ovens should be at the correct temperature before baking commences?

    ....

11 What are the potential hazards that may occur when using commercial ovens?

    ....

12 Rapid cooling is essential in the production of cakes, sponges and scones. Why?

    ....

13 At what temperatures should the following be baked?

Product	Temperature	Time
24–30 cm 10–12" Rich fruit cake		
Shortbread biscuits		
Sultana scones		
Swiss roll		
Queen cakes		
Victoria sandwich		

2ND9.3 *Decorate basic cakes, sponges and scones*

1 Before decorating products for service, it is important that:
   a Preparation areas and equipment are ready for use and satisfy health, safety and hygiene regulations.
   b Work is planned and time appropriately allocated to meet daily schedules.
   c Ingredients for fillings and decorations are of the type, quality and quantity required.
   d Fillings and decorations are suitably prepared for cake, sponge and scone decoration.
   e Cakes, sponges and scones are finished in accordance with product and customer requirements.
   f Cakes, sponges and scones are stored in accordance with food hygiene regulations.
   g Preparation areas and equipment are correctly cleaned after use.

2 Water icing (page 646, *Practical Cookery*).

3 Butter creams (pages 625–6, *Practical Cookery*).
   • When making uncooked butter cream, why is it important to sieve the icing sugar?

   ....

   • The icing sugar and butter must be creamed until light and fluffy or creamy. Can you overbeat this mixture? Yes or no? ....
      When flavouring and colouring butter cream, the golden rule should be to flavour gently, in other words to flavour lightly and to use colouring carefully to produce light, gentle colours. When using essences and colourings, they should never be poured directly from the bottle but poured into the bottle lid and then carefully added one or two drops at a time, mixing well in between and tasting and assessing the colour each time a few drops are added. Flavourings and colourings may also be added to mixtures with the aid of a pipette. (Examples of uses of butter cream, pages 712–3, *Practical Cookery*).
   • How is chocolate flavour and colour added for chocolate butter cream?

   ....

4 Royal icing (page 709, *Practical Cookery*).
   Royal icing is used in a variety of cakes, small and large. The most popular use is for celebration cakes, such as Christmas, christening and birthday cakes.

5 Whipped cream.
   • For cream to be able to be whipped, how much butterfat must it contain? ....
      When whipping cream, air is beaten in and the volume increases. When using a cream with the minimum of butterfat, maximum beating is possible and therefore the maximum volume can be obtained.

Caution: if cream is over-whipped it will separate, turn to butter and be unusable for decorating. Therefore, care must always be taken to prevent this happening.

• What would be the effect of whipping a thick double cream with 48% fat content?

....

• The ideal whipping cream contains 25%, 30%, 35%, 40% or 45% butterfat? ....
• There are four rules to be observed when whipping cream:
  1 It must be at room temperature or cold. Which is true? ....
  2 What is the best type of bowl to use: copper, china, plastic, metal or stainless steel? ....
  3 How can you prevent fresh cold cream from turning to butter when being whipped in hot conditions?

....

  4 What is the safest procedure for adding cream to hot liquids?

....

• Name six uses for whipped cream.

....

....

....

6 Terms used in the various methods of decorating:
  a Trimming refers to cutting the sponge or cake (if necessary) to make it even and symmetrical.
  b Filling applies to the filling of certain cakes, e.g. éclairs and profiteroles with a cream, or doughnuts with jam.
  c Spreading and smoothing are terms that are used when any icing or cream for decorating is used.
  d Piping with icing or chocolate. Making decorative lines, spirals, leaves, rosettes, etc., to achieve an attractive finish.
  e Piping with cream. The cream must be whipped until stiff, then placed into a piping bag, usually with a large star tube. The cream should be eased to the bottom of the bag and the top securely folded or twisted shut (if this is not done properly, the cream will ooze out of the top and on to the hands) before piping begins. To pipe, squeeze the bag gently but steadily with the right hand, and steady and guide the bag with the left hand.
     Whipped cream may be left plain, or it may be lightly sweetened and lightly flavoured with 2–3 drops of vanilla essence per 250 ml (½ pt) of cream and called Crême Chantilly.

f Dusting, dredging or sprinkling. This applies to the use of icing or castor sugar in a container with a perforated lid. It is also possible to form quick and artistic designs on certain cakes, e.g. chocolate cake, by cutting a simply patterned template the size of the cake out of white card, laying it on the cake, sprinkling generously with icing sugar and then carefully removing the template.

- Name three other cakes finished by sprinkling with castor sugar.

....

g Coating is completely covering the top of a large or small cake with an icing, butter cream or whipped cream. When applied, the coating should be carefully smoothed using a palette knife and, in some cases, with the cake on a turntable. For certain cakes, the sides are also coated.

h Topping is the final decoration, e.g. a glacé cherry or a strawberry or raspberry, on top of a rosette of whipped cream on a tartlet or a cream sponge.

- Name three other toppings.

....

7 State the differences in the following:

Royal icing   Water icing

....

Butter cream   Fondant

....

Commercial fondant

....

8 The contamination threats outlined on pages 43–50 of *Practical Cookery* are equally as relevant to the decoration of cakes and biscuits as to other foods.

9 Keeping preparation and storage areas and equipment hygienic is important. (Note carefully Food Hygiene Regulations 1990 with particular regard to storage temperatures.)

- Cream cakes must be stored at or below a temperature of 8°C (46°F). True or false?

....

10   Using the outline provided, design a finish to a plain Genoese gâteau, suggest a suitable filling. Use chocolate piping (fondant or butter cream). Ask your tutor or trainer for help.

11   State how the following is assessed for quality.

Product	Texture	Appearance	Flavour	Consistency
Water icing				
Chocolate butter cream	light creamy, smooth		good chocolate flavour	smooth, spreadable
Whipped cream			fresh	

12   Which products can you suggest could be used to substitute high fat ingredients when decorating basic cakes and sponges?

....

....

13   Why is it difficult to produce cakes and sponges of a quality that is acceptable to customers who are health conscious?

....

....

Record of Achievement – Completion of Unit 2ND9

Candidate's signature: _____

Assessor's signature: _____

Date: _____

Unit 2ND12

Prepare and cook basic pasta dishes

Read pages 215–235 of *Practical Cookery*.

1 Why is it important to keep preparation, cooking areas and equipment hygienic? Give examples of any bad practice that you may have observed.

....

....

2 What are the main contamination threats when preparing, cooking and storing pasta dishes?

....

....

3 How can the fibre content of pasta dishes be increased?

....

4 Before making and cooking pasta ensure that:
   a Preparation areas and equipment are ready for use and satisfy health, safety and hygiene regulations.
   b Work is planned and appropriate time allocated to meet daily schedules.
   c Ingredients are of the type, quality and quantity required.
   d Pasta is correctly prepared according to the dish requirements.
   e Prepared pasta not for immediate use is stored in accordance with food hygiene regulations, e.g. if fresh eggs are used in the making of fresh pasta, the fresher they are the longer the keeping quality of the pasta. When freshly made pasta is made for storage, it should be allowed to dry and be kept in a clean, dry container or bowl in a cool, dry store.
   f Pasta is correctly combined with other ingredients according to customer and dish requirements.
   g Pasta dishes are cooked and finished according to customer and dish requirements.
   h Preparation areas and equipment are correctly cleaned after use.

5 Always cook pasta in plenty of gently boiling salted water. Name the three other general points on the cooking and serving of pasta.

....

....

....

• What does the term *al dente* mean?

....

• Which cheese is traditionally served with pasta dishes?

....

• If wholewheat noodles are required, what proportion of wholewheat flour is added to the basic dough?

....

• Why after making pasta dough is it necessary to allow it to rest and relax?

....

• What spice may be used in a dish of buttered noodles?

....

• What is the approximate cooking time for meat ravioli, 5 min., 10 min. or
  15 min.? ....
• Name two sauces that could be served with meat ravioli.

....

• Other than the shape, what is the basic difference in the handling and cooking of pasta for ravioli and cannelloni?

....

....

• Name three types of pasta sheets that can be used in the making of a lasagne.

- Write out your idea for a non-meat lasagne.

  ....

  ....

  ....

- The number of pasta shapes available exceeds 10, 20, 30, 40 or 50 shapes?

  ....

6   The main contamination threats when preparing, cooking and storing pasta.
   a   The transfer of food poisoning bacteria by using the same preparation areas, equipment and utensils for preparing cooked and uncooked products.
   - Give an example.

     ....

   b   The transfer of food poisoning bacteria from unhygienic equipment, utensils and preparation methods.
   - Give an example.

     ....

   c   The transfer of food poisoning bacteria from the mouth, nose, open cuts and sores and unclean hands to food.
   - Give an example.

     ....

   d   Uncovered food contaminated by pests carrying bacteria.
   - Give an example.

     ....

   e   Not disposing of waste or storing unused items in the correct manner.
   - Give an example.

     ....

7   It is important to keep preparation and storage areas and equipment hygienic.
   a   To prevent contamination of food by food poisoning bacteria.
   - Give an example.

     ....

b To prevent pest infestation and unpleasant odours arising.
- Give an example.

....

c To ensure that standards of cleanliness are maintained.
- Give an example.

....

d To comply with the law.
- Give an example.

....

8 Time and temperature are important in the cooking of fresh pasta:
   a To ensure correctly cooked pasta and pasta dishes, e.g. if pasta is not cooked in ample gently boiling water it will clog together; and if pasta is overcooked it will become soft and mushy.
   - To what degree should pasta be cooked?

....

   b To prevent food poisoning, e.g. if undercooked fresh egg pasta is allowed to remain warm in a warm kitchen for a considerable period of time food poisoning bacteria could multiply.
   c To ensure that the loss of nutritional value of prepared food is minimised, e.g. keeping prepared food warm for long periods will result in nutritional loss, therefore reheat pasta and combine the ingredients quickly and serve immediately.
   d Prepared cooked pasta may also be kept in a vacuum pack and stored under refrigeration for several days.

Record of Achievement – Completion of Unit 2ND12

Candidate's signature: _____

Assessor's signature: _____

Date: _____

Unit 2ND18

Prepare and cook vegetables for basic hot dishes and salads

2ND18.1 *Prepare vegetables for hot dishes and salads*

Read pages 517–580 of *Practical Cookery*.

1 Certain vegetables may be packed in heavy containers. What are the correct and safe lifting methods?

....

....

2 What are the main contamination threats when preparing and storing raw vegetables?

....

....

3 Why should washed vegetables be kept separate from unwashed vegetables?

....

4 Why must all vegetables be thoroughly washed?

....

5 For and during the preparation of vegetables, it is important to ensure that:
  a Preparation areas and equipment are ready for use and satisfy health, safety and hygiene requirements.
  b Vegetables are of the type, quality and quantity required.
  c Vegetables are prepared according to dish and customer requirements.
  d Prepared vegetables not for immediate use are stored in accordance with food hygiene regulations.
  e Preparation areas and equipment are correctly cleaned after use.
  f Unexpected situations are reported and dealt with in accordance with laid-down procedures.
  g Appropriate action is taken to deal with unexpected situations within an individual's responsibility.

h All work is carried out in an organised and efficient manner taking account of priorities and laid-down procedures.

6 Vegetables.
  • Complete the following table by adding three examples to each vegetable type.

Classification	1	2	3	4
Roots	carrots			
Tubers	potatoes			
Bulbs	onions			
Leaves	spinach			
Brassicas	cabbage			
Pods and seeds	sweetcorn			
Fruiting	tomatoes			
Stems and shoots	celery			
Fungi	mushrooms			
Frozen/convenience	peas			
Vegetable-protein	TVP			

7 Storage.
Fresh vegetables are living organisms and will lose quality quickly if not correctly stored and handled after being harvested. It follows therefore that when fresh vegetables have been delivered to the kitchen, they should be handled and stored carefully. Roots, tubers and bulbs should be emptied from their containers and stored in bins or racks in a cool, well-ventilated store. They should be checked, and any unsound vegetables should be discarded.

Leafy vegetables, brassicas, pods and seeds (sometimes known as legumes), fruiting vegetables, stems and shoots and fungi ideally should be ordered, delivered and used daily, so that they spend the minimum time in store. If this is done and provided they are cooked correctly, then they will retain the maximum food value. In practice many of these vegetables will be stored overnight or for a few days. In all cases, they should be checked daily and any unsound vegetables discarded. Most of these vegetables are kept in a cool, well-ventilated store and, in some cases, e.g. lettuce, tomatoes and fungi, in a refrigerator.

8 Why is it important to follow suppliers' instructions on storing frozen vegetables?

....

9 Why should blemished vegetables be stored separately from perfect produce?

....

10 Why should vegetables be removed or loosened from plastic wrapping?

....

11 Which preparation techniques can increase fibre in vegetable dishes? Give examples.

....

....

12 List the quality points to look for in fresh vegetables.

....

....

....

13 What preparation methods are suitable for different types of vegetables? Set out your answer in the form of a chart.

....

....

....

....

....

14 Methods of preparation (pages 522–580, *Practical Cookery*).
- List the five stages of making a vegetable purée.

....

....

....

- If the vegetable to be puréed has to be cut up, why is it important to cut it into roughly uniform pieces?

  ....

  ....

- Why should the vegetables only be barely covered with water?

  ....

- Name four vegetables suitable for puréeing.

  ....

  ....

- In order to give a neat presentation, puréed vegetables may be set into moulds.
- For a hot vegetable purée to be neatly turned out of a mould and retain its shape, the mould must be correctly prepared. It must be .... and lightly greased with .... or ....

2ND18.2 *Cook vegetables for basic hot dishes and salads*

Read pages 517–580 of *Practical Cookery*.

1   What are the correct and safe methods of lifting heavy containers of vegetables?

  ....

  ....

2   List the main contamination threats when cooking vegetable dishes?

  ....

  ....

3   Why is it important to keep cooking areas and equipment hygienic?

  ....

  ....

4   Why are time and temperature important when cooking vegetable dishes?

....

....

5   Why should vegetables be boiled gently?

....

6   What are the benefits of sweating certain vegetables gently?

....

7   What cooking methods minimise nutritional loss?

....

8   What preparation and cooking methods cut down on the oil absorbed by potatoes when deep frying?

....

9   Why is it important to minimise salt added to vegetables?

....

10   Before cooking and finishing vegetable dishes the following must be observed:
   a Cooking areas and equipment are ready for use and satisfy health, safety and food hygiene regulations.
   b Vegetables are of the type, quality and quantity required.
   c Vegetables are correctly combined with other ingredients and cooked according to customer and dish requirements.
   d Prepared vegetable dishes are finished using the presentation methods appropriate to customer and dish requirements.
   e Finished vegetables not for immediate consumption are stored in accordance with laid-down procedures.
   f Cooking areas and equipment are correctly cleaned after use.
   g Unexpected situations are reported and dealt with in accordance with laid-down procedures.
   h Appropriate action is taken to deal with unexpected situations within the individual's responsibility.
   i All work is carried out in an organised and efficient manner taking account of priorities and laid-down procedures.

- Name two vegetables that are often roasted.

  ....

- What are the two ways in which parsnips can be roasted?

  ....

- When roasting potatoes or parsnips, heating the fat or oil before adding the vegetables lessens the chances of them sticking to the tray. True or false? ....
- Why must potatoes which are to be roasted be well dried on all sides before putting into the hot fat?

  ....

- What is the most suitable oven temperature for roasting potatoes: moderate, hot or very hot? ....
- Why is it best to turn roast potatoes and parsnips over when they are half cooked?

  ....

- When roast potatoes or parsnips are cooked, they must be well .... before serving.
- Describe the method of preparing, cooking and serving baked jacket potatoes.

  ....

  ....

- Baked jacket potatoes can be served as a snack meal with a variety of fillings. Name four fillings which you have seen and then suggest a filling of your choice.

  ....

  ....

  ....

  ....

- Baked jacket potatoes can also be scooped out, the cooked potato processed and cooked. Briefly describe three different ways of varying this dish.

  ....

  ....

  ....

  ....

- Outline the preparation, cooking and serving of grilled tomatoes and grilled mushrooms.

  ....

  ....

  Numerous vegetables can be cooked by shallow frying (Brussels sprouts, cauliflower, chicory, courgettes, onions: pages 536–545; potatoes: pages 569–570; *Practical Cookery*).
- Golden rules when shallow frying vegetables:
  1 ensure the pan is ....;
  2 use a good clean fat or ....;
  3 heat the fat or .... before adding the vegetables;
  4 cook to an appetising light .... on both sides;
  5 .... lightly;
  6 finally add a light sprinkle of freshly chopped ....
- For which of the previous list of fried vegetables are the vegetables pre-cooked by boiling or steaming?

  ....

- For which of the above list of vegetables are the vegetables pre-cooked by baking?

  ....

- Which of the above list of vegetables are cooked by frying on both sides and which are cooked by sautéeing?

  ....

- What is meant by the term sautéeing?

  ....

- Those vegetables which are cooked on both sides only may alternatively be cooked on a clean, lightly greased griddle, e.g. tomatoes and ....
  Many vegetables can also be stir fried (page 533, *Practical Cookery*).
- As stir fry vegetables should only take approximately 3 min. to cook, they must be cut into .... pieces.
- How can a good green colour be retained in green vegetables when they are to be stir fried?

  ....

- As a general rule, all root vegetables are started to cook in .... salted water; those vegetables which grow above the ground are started in .... salted water.
- What is the reason for cooking green vegetables in this way?

  ....

- What is a quicker way of cooking vegetables than boiling?

  ....

- What are the advantages of cooking vegetables for as short a time as possible?

  ....

- What are the four factors which affect the cooking time of vegetables?

  ....

  ....

- The golden rules of boiling vegetables are:
  1 ensure they are of a .... size;
  2 use a pan of suitable size, neither too .... or ....;
  3 .... with water;
  4 lightly season with ....;
  5 cook for the .... time possible;
  6 drain off well (most vegetable cooking liquids can be used for vegetable stock if required);
  7 dry off if necessary, e.g. ....;
  8 serve as soon as possible.
- Why should aluminium pans not be used for braising red cabbage?

  ....

- When braising celery, what is the reason for blanching it first?

  ....

- When braising leeks, why are they tied into bunches after having been washed and before they are cooked?

  ....

- An example of cooking vegetables by stewing is ratatouille. List the ingredients and outline the method for making a dish of ratatouille.

Ingredients	*Method*
courgettes	....
aubergines	....

....

....

....

- Give two other examples of vegetables which can be cooked by stewing.

....

- All vegetables cooked by boiling may also be steamed. The vegetables are prepared exactly the same as for boiling and then placed into steamer trays, lightly seasoned with salt and steamed under pressure for the minimum period of time in order to conserve maximum food .... and retain c........................ .
Modern high-pressure steamers are ideal for this purpose (pages 86–89, *Practical Cookery*).
   Many vegetables can be deep fried including courgettes, onion rings, salsify, mixed fried vegetables, (pages 539, 545, 548, 554 *Practical Cookery*). Then a wide range of potato dishes and shapes, e.g. crisps, croquettes, chips, matchsticks, (pages 566 and 570–1, *Practical Cookery*) can also be deep fried.
- Vegetables for deep frying are passed through a light ....
- French-style fried onions are passed through .... and ....
- What is the difference between onions fried English and French styles?

....

- Suggest a selection of six vegetables that could be served in a mixed vegetable stir fry.

....

....

- The frying temperature for vegetables is: 160°C, 170°C, 180°C, 190°C or 200°C (pages 102–105, *Practical Cookery*)? ....
- What is the term used for the partial cooking of fried potatoes?

....

- What is the purpose of partial cooking of fried potatoes?

....

- What is meant by the following terms?
  Coating: ....

  Draining: ....

  Holding for service: ....

  Spider: ....
- Why must fryers never be overfilled with fat, oil or the food to be fried?

  ....

- If smoke arises from a deep fat fryer, this is a danger sign of what? What should immediately be done?

  ....

- Why should the frying fat or oil be strained after each use?

  ....

- Why should fryers be covered when not in use?

  ....

  As accidents using deep fat fryers are common in many kitchens it is important that you read and understand the rules of safety on page 105, *Practical Cookery*.
- Why must foods to be fried be well dried?

  ....

- When placing food in a fryer, e.g. pieces of fish, why must they always be placed in away and not towards you?

  ....

- Why is it important to have a spider and basket to hand when deep-frying food?

  ....

- Why should the jacket sleeves always be rolled down when frying foods?

  ....

11 Certain dishes of vegetables are finished by browning, e.g. cauliflower au gratin (page 537, *Practical Cookery*). Other vegetables that can be finished in the same way include broccoli, sea-kale and marrow.

There are various methods of finishing vegetables:

a Glazing: when cooked vegetables such as carrots and turnips are tossed in butter over a fierce heat to give them a shine (page 529, *Practical Cookery*).

b Coating: this is when vegetables, e.g. cauliflower, are coated with a sauce before serving. Also braised vegetables are coated with a light sauce made from the cooking liquid (e.g. page 531, *Practical Cookery*).

c Colouring: this can be carried out by shallow or deep frying, placing under the salamander or in the oven.

d Using hot sauces: in certain cases, the sauce may be poured over the vegetable; in others, it is best to serve it separately, e.g. if warm Hollandaise sauce is placed over hot broccoli in the kitchen it may curdle.

e Using cold sauces: sauces such as mayonnaise or vinaigrette when served with cold asparagus are best served separately.

f Garnishing: with most vegetable dishes, little or no garnishing is required as the vegetable colours are sufficient. A little chopped parsley on, for example, sauté potatoes or savoury potatoes, may be used.

g Piping: usually with duchesse type potatoes (page 566, *Practical Cookery*).

12 Draw the presentation of some vegetable dishes you have recently been involved with, e.g. purée of swede (scroll finish), braised celery (celery head, jus lié).

Record of Achievement – Completion of Unit 2ND18

Candidate's signature: _____

Assessor's signature: _____

Date: _____

Unit 2ND19

Prepare and cook basic vegetable protein dishes

2ND19.1 *Prepare basic vegetable protein dishes*

Read page 295 in *Practical Cookery*.

Vegetable protein recipes are designed to produce a high protein dish often used as a substitute for meat. As the number of vegetarians increases, so does the need to create new high protein substitutes for meat.

Examples of alternative products are:
Quorn
Textured vegetable protein
Tofu

Textured vegetable protein is produced in a number of varieties. Pulses and vegetables contribute a valuable source of protein to a number of vegetable dishes.

1 Name four different types of textured vegetable protein.

    ....

    ....

    ....

    ....

2 What is the basic ingredient of tofu? (Page 749, *Practical Cookery*)

    ....

3 Quorn is a name given to a special vegetable protein product. What is the basis of this product?

    ....

4   Name two dishes you are familiar with which can be produced from:
    Quorn: ....
    Tofu: ....

5   Name two fresh vegetables which are a good source of protein.

    ....

6   Cereals, nuts and seeds are also good sources of protein. Give examples of each
    which you are familiar with.
    Cereals:

    ....

    ....

    Nuts:

    ....

    ....

    Seeds:

    ....

    ....

7   Name six preserved vegetables or fruit which may be used in a vegetable protein dish.

    ....

    ....

8   List the characteristics you would look for when inspecting fresh vegetables.

    ....

    ....

    ....

9   What are the main problems which have to be considered when preparing large
    quantities of vegetable protein dishes?

    ....

10 When assessing the quality of a vegetable protein dish, flavour and texture is very important. Why are aroma, consistency and appearance also important?

....

11 What hygiene and safety have to be considered when preparing vegetable protein dishes?

....

12 Which ingredients for vegetable protein dishes have to be soaked?

....

13 List the various preparation methods which you are familiar with when preparing vegetable protein dishes:
chopping
slicing

....

....

....

....

14 At what temperature should vegetable protein dishes be served?

....

15 State the quality points you would look for in the following:
Textured vegetable protein:

....

....

Tofu:

....

....

Mycoprotein:

....

....

16 Write down a recipe for four people suitable for vegetarians who are also on a low cholesterol diet.

....

....

....

....

....

....

....

....

....

17 Why is fibre an important contribution to a balanced diet?

....

18 List six ingredients high in fibre.

....

....

....

19 Why do some chefs reduce the salt in vegetable protein dishes?

....

20 Tofu is used extensively in which type of cuisine?

....

2ND19.2 *Cook basic vegetable protein dishes*

1 Name a suitable vegetable protein dish cooked by one of the following methods:
grilling ....
shallow frying ....
stir frying ....
boiling ....
braising   stewed cabbage with rice, pine kernels and peppers
stewing ....
deep frying   tempura vegetables
roasting ....
baking ....

2 Choose a vegetable protein dish. Describe the characteristics of this dish according to the following:
Name of dish: ....
Texture: ....
Flavour: ....
Aroma: ....
Appearance: ....
Consistency: ....

3 List any small or large equipment you require to produce the dish you selected.

....

....

4 List any hygiene, health and safety precautions you have to consider when preparing your named dish.

....

....

5 Compile a four course vegetarian menu, describing each dish of your choice.

....

....

....

....

....

....

....

....

....

....

6 List eight types of fat/oil which may be used in vegetarian dishes.
Sunflower oil ....
Rape seed oil ....
Walnut seed ....

....

7 Explain why time and temperature is important when cooking basic vegetable protein dishes.

....

....

8 List the vegetable protein dishes you have recently prepared.

....

....

Record of Achievement – Completion of Unit 2ND19

Candidate's signature: _____

Assessor's signature: _____

Date: _____

Prepare and cook basic egg dishes

2ND10.1 *Prepare and cook basic egg dishes*

Read pages 198–212 of *Practical Cookery*.

1   Why is it important to keep preparation, cooking and storage areas and equipment hygienic? Give examples of any bad practice that you may have observed.

....

....

....

....

2   What are the main contamination threats when cooking and finishing egg dishes?

....

....

....

3   What are the storage/holding requirements for eggs?

....

4   Why should eggs be stored away from strong smelling foods such as onions, fish and cheese?

....

5   What is the basic nutritional value of eggs?

....

6 If hens' eggs were unobtainable, which other two birds' eggs could be used?

....

7 List the quality points for eggs.

....

....

8 List the signs of staleness in eggs when they are broken.

....

....

9 Name the bacteria which has affected some eggs causing food poisoning.

....

10 Which two groups of people are most likely to be affected by this bacteria?

....

....

11 Pasteurised eggs are available. How is this process carried out and for what purpose?

....

....

12 Describe the appearance of the yolk in a fresh egg.

....

13 Describe the appearance of the white of a stale egg.

....

14 What is the effect on scrambled eggs if they are cooked too quickly or for too long?

....

....

15 If scrambled eggs have to be prepared in bulk, what is the advantage of using pasteurised eggs?

....

....

16 When preparing small quantities of scrambled eggs, why should the pan be removed from the heat before the eggs are finally cooked?

....

....

17 The cooking time for eggs in cocotte is 1–2 min., 2–3 min., 3–4 min. or 4–5 min.? ....

18 Boiled eggs require how much cooking time:
    a When started in cold water and after coming to the boil .... min.?
    b When plunged into boiling water and coming to the boil .... min.?

19 Describe the cooking of soft boiled eggs to be served with the shells removed.

....

....

20 Hard boiled eggs plunged into boiling water and re-boiled require 6–8 min., 9–11 min. or 12–14 min. cooking time? ....

21 When a hard boiled egg is cut in half what shows:
    that the egg is fresh? ....
    that the egg is not overcooked? ....

22 List the various ingredients that can be used for frying eggs. Which are the healthiest?

....

....

....

23 What would be the difference in the final appearance of a poached egg:
using a fresh egg? ....
using a stale egg? ....
Explain this difference.

....

....

....

....

24 What is the reason for adding a little vinegar to the water when poaching eggs?

....

....

•   What would be the effects of using too much vinegar?

....

....

25 When serving poached eggs on toast, what is the last essential thing that should be done to the eggs, after removing them from the water and before placing them on toast?

....

....

26 A Spanish omelet is traditional served flat. Suggest six variations of flat omelets:

....

....

....

....

....

....

27 What is the difference between the finished appearance of:

a savoury omelet: ....

....

a jam omelet: ....

....

28 What is the price of twelve size 3 eggs? ....

Record of Achievement – Completion of Unit 2ND10

Candidate's signature: _____

Assessor's signature: _____

Date: _____

Receive, handle and store food deliveries

2ND11.1 *Receive food deliveries*

Information on this unit will be found in *Theory of Catering*, 8th Edition.

1   Why should receiving and storage areas be prepared ready for delivery?

    ....

2   Why is it important that all food orders be checked on delivery?

    ....

3   Foods purchased should be of the right quality required. Why should they not exceed the expiry date?

    ....

4   Two documents are required to check food deliveries, one is the order that has been given. What is the name of the other document that the delivery person will bring?

    ....

5   When foods are delivered they should meet the requirements, and the food packaging must be undamaged. What should you do if food arrives in damaged containers?

    ....

    ....

6   How should receiving areas be kept?

    ....

    ....

7   What do you understand by unauthorised access?

    ....

8   There are four reasons why receiving areas should be secured from unauthorised access. Two of them are to prevent accidents and injury, and to prevent vandalism to receiving areas and items. What are the other two?

....

....

9   How should delivery problems be dealt with?

....

10 State your establishment's procedures for dealing with food deliveries.

....

....

....

11 What are the legal requirements for dealing with receiving and storing food?

....

....

....

12 Why is it important that all work is planned and time is appropriately allocated to meet daily schedules?

....

13 What should be the procedure if some foods in a delivery are damaged or exceed the sell-by date?

....

14 If any of the items delivered have to be returned because of damage, lack of freshness, quality or any other reason, what document should the delivery person sign before taking the items away?

....

15 If deliveries of chilled or frozen foods are made, the temperatures must be checked to ensure that they comply with the temperatures laid down by your employer and then the food must be swiftly transferred to the correct storage cabinets.
- Once food has been received and signed for it must be handled carefully while it is being transferred to storage cabinets.
- Delivery documentation must be correctly completed. There are at least two and sometimes three documents used. What are these?

....

....

....

16 Define what you understand by quality.

....

....

17 Food packaging refers to boxes, wooden and cardboard, and cans. Name three types of food packaging.

....

....

....

18 Why is it important to keep all receiving areas clean, tidy and free from rubbish?

....

19 How many different storage areas would be required for the correct storage of chilled, frozen, cooked, uncooked, preserved and ambient foods and why?

....

....

20 What is the meaning of the word ambient?

....

21 Who in your establishment or institution is responsible for checking the incoming goods?

....

- Who else in your establishment has responsibility for incoming goods?

....

- How often are the chill rooms and cold rooms in this area checked?
  a Daily ☐
  b Weekly ☐
  c Monthly ☐
  d Never ☐
- Before any food supplier becomes a designated supplier of food commodities to your establishment in the case of perishable foods, it is advisable for a member of the management team to visit the premises. Why?

....

....

- Meat suppliers under the Food Safety Act are required to deliver meat in refrigerated vans. Why?

....

- Check: does the butcher who delivers to your premises use refrigerated transport?

....

22 Each establishment should have a system of recording, ordering, delivery and distribution of food. This system includes a means of checking deliveries against orders, recording quantities of stock and the amounts issued and to whom.
- Describe the system in your establishment.

....

....

....

....

23 Why should a constant flow of stock be maintained?

....

24 Before items are delivered, it is necessary to know what has been ordered, both the amount and quality and when it will be delivered.

The procedure for accepting deliveries is as follows:

ensure adequate store space is available;

ensure access to the space is clear;

check .... of goods where appropriate;

check perishable goods immediately;

ensure there is no .... in transporting items to cold storage;

check all other goods for .... and ...., then store;

return any .... items;

do not accept items past their 'use by' or 'best before' dates;

ensure .... or amended delivery notes record returns;

return one part of the .... note;

ensure the other part is kept by the ....;

ensure that a .... note is provided for any goods not delivered;

Should there be any discrepancies, who do you inform?

....

25 Why should procedures be laid down for checking the temperatures of foods on arrival?

....

....

26 List four perishable foods and four semi-perishable foods.

....

....

....

....

2ND11.2 *Store food deliveries*

1 What do you understand as a food type. Name four food types.

....

....

2 A constant stock of food items should always be maintained to maintain efficiency in the workplace and to maintain sales levels.
 • Give two more reasons:

 ....

 ....

 • What documents are used for receiving, storing and issuing food items?

 ....

 ....

 • Food items should only be issued from the stores on receipt of what?

 ....

 • If any food stocks are low, to whom should it be reported?

 ....

3 There are five reasons why correct storage and rotation procedures for all foods should be followed: three of them are: to ensure correct temperature of food items is maintained, to ensure food is used in date order or order of quality specifications, and to prevent damage to, and contamination of, products.
 • Give two more reasons:

 ....

 ....

4 Good record keeping is essential. Why?

 ....

 ....

5 Describe the following:
 An invoice: ....
 Statement: ....
 Purchase order: ....

6 All food storage areas must be regularly cleaned and kept in an orderly fashion.
 • Why is this important in relation to health and safety legislation and food hygiene?

 ....

 ....

7 Cross contamination can be a major problem in food spoilage. Why?

....

....

8 Stock control is a wide ranging term which includes:
  a setting stockholders' levels
  b recording ....
  c physical ....
  • Why is stock control important?

....

....

....

  • What is the purpose of stocktaking?

....

....

  • What steps could you take if the stock results are unfavourable?
  a minimise number of key holders
  b physical check of deliveries on arrival
  c check and measure portion controls
  d check waste
  • Name three other steps you might take.

....

....

....

9 What legislation covers the storage of food?

....

10 What dangers are associated with pest infestation?

....

11 How should frozen and chilled food be dealt with on arrival?

....

12 Why is ventilation and temperature important when storing food?

....

13 Why should access to the food be restricted?

....

14 Name two types of containers suitable for storing food.

....

....

15 What do the following symbols denote?

* ....

** ....

*** ....

**** ....

16 What criticism, if any, do you have of your establishment's food stores?

....

....

Record of Achievement – Completion of Unit 2ND11

Candidate's signature: _____

Assessor's signature: _____

Date: _____

Unit 2ND13

Prepare and present food for cold presentation

2ND13.1 *Prepare and present sandwiches and canapés*

Read pages 739–742 of *Practical Cookery*.

1 Name six types of bread which may be used for open sandwiches.
   1 French sticks
   2 ....
   3 ....
   4 ....
   5 ....
   6 ....

2 State what the current legislation is for storage of sandwiches.

   ....

3 State why time and temperature is important when preparing and presenting sandwiches and canapés.

   ....

4 What is considered to be a safe temperature for storing sandwiches and canapés if they are not for immediate consumption?

   ....

5 Open sandwiches (page 742, *Practical Cookery*) are popular in Scandinavian countries and an appetising variety is usually available at almost any time of day when they are eaten as a snack, as part of a meal or as a main meal according to the customer's taste and requirements.
   Open sandwiches are traditionally made with buttered thin slices of wholemeal bread on which are generously piled good helpings of freshly prepared raw and cooked foods. It is important that they always appear fresh and appetising and should therefore be prepared as close to service time as possible.

- Once open sandwiches are prepared, where should they be kept prior to and during service?

  ....

6 Name four quality points you would look for when assessing open sandwiches.

  ....

  ....

  ....

  ....

7 The main contamination threats when preparing and storing canapés and open sandwiches are:

  a The transfer of food poisoning bacteria by using the same preparation areas, equipment and utensils for preparing cooked and uncooked products.
  - Give an example.

  ....

  b The transfer of food poisoning bacteria from unhygienic utensils, equipment and preparation areas.
  - Give an example.

  ....

  c The transfer of food poisoning bacteria from the mouth, nose, open cuts and sores and unclean hands to food.
  - Give an example.

  ....

  d Uncovered food contaminated by pests carrying bacteria.
  - Give an example.

  ....

  e Not disposing of waste or storing unused items in the correct manner.
  - Give an example.

  ....

8 It is important to keep preparation and storage areas and equipment hygienic to:
   a Prevent contamination of food by food poisoning bacteria.
   • Give an example.

   ....

   b Prevent pest infestation and unpleasant odours arising.
   • Give an example.

   ....

   c Ensure that standards of cleanliness are maintained.
   • Give an example.

   ....

   d Comply with the law.

9 Suggest six different foods suitable for placing on bases to make canapés.

   ....

   ....

   • After preparing canapés what are three ways in which they may be finished?

   ....

   ....

   • Suggest four fish suitable for canapés on bases.

   ....

   • Make a list of six types of canapés which may be served hot and six that may be served cold.

Hot	Cold
....	....
....	....
....	....
....	....
....	....
....	....

- Name four varieties of hot canapés you have recently prepared.

....

....

- Why is it important that hot canapés are bite-sized?

....

10 Vol-au-vents are large puff pastry cases usually made to a size suitable either for a first course, e.g. chicken and mushroom, or a fish course, e.g. sea-food in white wine sauce, or as a main course (page 284, *Practical Cookery*). The small bite-sized puff pastry cases served as canapés are known as bouchées, which is a French word meaning mouthful.

11 Bouchées may be served hot or cold and are usually referred to as cocktail savouries, along with many other items, such as baby pizzas and fried fish goujons.

12 Name three more substitutes to high fat ingredients when preparing sandwiches and canapés:
Low fat spread

....

....

....

13 When preparing open sandwiches and canapés, what fats/oils can contribute to healthier catering practices?

....

....

....

14 Name four ingredients which can increase the fibre intake when consuming open sandwiches and canapés.

....

....

....

....

2ND13.2 *Present cooked, cured and prepared foods*

Read pages 155–196 of *Practical Cookery*.

1 Why is hygiene of particular importance when dealing with cold food?

   ....

2 Appearance of cold food must be clean and fresh. Briefly describe how rules should
   be applied to presentation.

   ....

   ....

3 Why is it advisable that foods taken from the 'fridge are allowed to stand at room
   temperature for 5–10 mins before being served?

   ....

   ....

4 Name the three categories of hors d'oeuvre.

   ....

   ....

   ....

5 Describe a basic salad you have prepared previously.

   ....

6 Potted shrimps are commonly known as a commercially prepared hors d'oeuvre. Name three others.

....

7 What special precautions should be taken into account when serving pre-prepared terrines and pâtés?

....

....

8 Give an example of when you may be required to use a chaudfroid sauce.

....

9 Special care must be taken by the chef when using aspic jelly. Why?

....

10 Name three different types of shellfish which may be served cold.

....

11 Name four cured meats which may be served as a first course.

....

....

12 What special precautions need to be taken into account when serving cold chicken?

....

....

13 Name three shellfish cocktail. Briefly describe the preparation of one of them.

....

....

....

14 Name eight hors-d'oeuvre suitable for an hors-d'oeuvre trolley. Arrange them below to give maximum presentational effect.

**Egg
mayonnaise**

---

15 Describe the presentation of sliced cold meats for a buffet table.

....

....

16 Parma, Bayonne and Ardennes are imported hams. Name two British hams.

....

17 Raised pies can provide the chef with particular problems related to food storage and hygiene. Why?

....

....

18 What safe working practices does your establishment employ when preparing cooked, cured and prepared foods?

....

....

19 State the main contamination threats that need to be considered when preparing and storing cooked, cured and prepared foods for presentation.

....

....

20 When preparing cooked and cured food, why is the relationship of time and temperature important?

....

21 At what temperature should cold food for consumption be stored before and during presentation?

....

22 Presentation is considered to be an important indicator of quality, especially for cold buffet service. Name three other quality points you should look for.

....

....

....

23 Suggest how the fat content of cold items could be reduced.

....

24 When making mayonnaise and vinegarette, suggest which oils could be used to give a low cholesterol product.

....

25 Suggest ways in which the fibre content of cold buffet items could be increased.

....

26 Should a chef consider reducing the amount of salt in prepared items? If yes, why?

....

27 What legal requirements apply to the preparation and service of cold buffet items?

....

28 How should food which has been returned from the buffet table be dealt with?

....

29 What is meant by a daily schedule?

....

30 What is the purpose of a sneeze screen?

....

31 Dishes prepared in advance should be covered with film and refrigerated at 1–3°C. Why?

....

32 If you were slicing cold meat from the remaining half of a 3½ kilo (7 lb) joint of beef which had previously been served hot, what would you do with the first slice and why?

....

....

- When preparing joints to be carved in front of the customer, why is it important to remove certain bones first?

....

- Why when preparing a joint to be stuffed, e.g. loin of lamb, is it important to bone out the joint, add the stuffing and then roll and tie the joint?

....

- Why is it desirable to cut meat for serving cold as near to service time as possible?

....

....

- If cold meat is to be cut and presented for 500 people, what procedures would be adopted to prevent the meat from drying up and looking unappetising?

....

....

- Describe how a joint of roast beef can be presented.

....

- Before a turkey is roasted for service cold, what bone should be removed and why?

....

- When preparing a turkey for roasting and serving cold, is it a good idea to remove the legs, bone and stuff them and roast them separately? Give reasons for your answer.

....

....

....

....

....

• When whole hams or joints of gammon are boiled for cold service, when should they be cooked, how should they be allowed to cool and where should they be stored?

....

....

....

• If cold roast chicken is to be served moist and succulent for lunch at one o'clock, when should they be cooked?

....

• In to how many pieces is a 1¼–1½ kg (2½–3 lb) chicken usually carved? What constitutes a portion?

....

33 Popular fish or shellfish on cold buffet include:
Salmon either whole or cut in portions (pages 189–91, *Practical Cookery*).
Crab (page 278, *Practical Cookery*).
Lobster (page 276, *Practical Cookery*).
Oysters (page 165, *Practical Cookery*).
Smoked fish (page 246, *Practical Cookery*).
Shellfish cocktails (page 170, *Practical Cookery*).
   If a salmon is to be presented and served cold from the whole fish, what is the procedure?

....

....

....

....

- What sauce is generally offered with cold salmon? ....
- Name four ways in which salmon may be served cold.

....

....

- What is the name given to a slice of salmon cut on the bone?
- After cooking slices of salmon on the bone for serving cold, remove the centre ...., all .... and ....
- When removing all the brown meat from the shell of a crab, what two parts should be discarded?

....

- How is the brown meat prepared?

....

- How is the shape of the crab shell neatened?

....

- Once neatened, what should be done to the crab shell before dressing the meat back in?

....

- After cutting a cooked lobster in half, what two parts should be removed before serving?

....

....

Record of Achievement – Completion of Unit 2ND13

Candidate's signature: _____

Assessor's signature: _____

Date: _____

Unit 2ND14

Prepare and cook basic shellfish dishes

2ND14.1 *Prepare basic shellfish dishes*

Read pages 274–284 of *Practical Cookery*.

1   State the quality points you should look for when purchasing shellfish.

    ....

    ....

2   Why should lobster, crab, mussels and oysters be purchased live whenever possible?

    ....

    ....

3   When preparing and cooking shellfish it is important to see that:
    a Preparation and cooking areas and equipment are ready for use and satisfy health,
       safety and hygiene regulations.
    b Work is planned and time appropriately allocated to meet daily schedules.
    c Shellfish are of the type, quality and quantity required.
    d Shellfish are suitably prepared for the cooking process.
    e Shellfish are cooked according to customer and dish requirements.
    f Shellfish are finished according to customer and dish requirements.
    g Prepared shellfish not for immediate consumption is stored in accordance with
       food hygiene regulations.
    h Preparation and cooking areas and equipment are correctly cleaned after use.

4   What is meant by the following preparation terms?
    Trimming: ....

    Shelling: ....

    Debearding: ....

    Scraping: ....

Cleaning: ....

Coating: ....

5 Why is it important to maintain hygienic and safe working practices when preparing shellfish dishes?

....

....

6 What are the main contamination threats that must be considered when preparing and storing basic shellfish dishes?

....

....

7 State why time and temperature is important when preparing basic shellfish dishes.

....

8 At what temperature should:
raw shellfish be stored? ....
shellfish be served cold? ....
hot shellfish be served? ....
• Lobster mornay contains a rich cheese sauce high in fat. Suggest ways in which the fat content can be reduced.

....

9 Suggest ways in which the fibre content of shellfish dishes can be increased.

....

10 Shellfish.
• Why must cockles be soaked in salt water before cooking?

....

2ND1.2 *Cook basic shellfish dishes*

1 Name a shellfish dish cooked by:
   a the dry method ....

b the wet method ....
- How would these dishes appear on the menu?

....

2 Give three examples of shellfish dishes cooked by:
Deep frying ....
Shallow frying ....
Poaching ....
Boiling ....

3 When deep frying shellfish what do you understand as the flash point and at what
approximate temperature does it occur?

....

4 Great care must be taken relating to the hygiene of cooking areas and equipment
when cooking shellfish dishes. List four points to look for.

a Raw shellfish should not come into contact with cooked shellfish, thus preventing
cross contamination.

b ....

....

c ....

....

d ....

....

5 How can you distinguish prawns from shrimps?

....

- Suggest three uses for prawns.

....

Prawns may be purchased uncooked and cooked by grilling, barbecuing, steaming,
boiling or stir-frying.

- What is the difference between crawfish and crayfish?

  ....

- What is the difference between crawfish and langoustine?

  ....

- What two other names are langoustine sometimes called?

  ....

- What is a popular use for crawfish, and why?

  ....

  ....

- The tail meat of crawfish can be used in the same way as the tail meat from lobsters. True or false? ....
- Lobsters and crabs have two claws. How many claws are on a crawfish? ....
- Crab meat is popular in many cold dishes, suggest six ways in which it may be used.

  ....

  ....

  ....

- When buying mussels, what four quality points should be looked for?

  ....

6 Cooking shellfish (page 277, *Practical Cookery*).
- When cooking shellfish should they be plunged into cold or boiling salted water?

  ....

- After the white meat has been removed from a crab, it is shredded. What is the best way to do this to avoid leaving small pieces of shell?

  ....

- If you were required to prepare and serve six portions of dressed crab, would you dress six small crabs or one large one? Give reasons for your choice.

……………………………………………………………………………………………………

There are numerous ways of serving lobster hot, e.g. soup, bouchées, vol-au-vent and pasties, in which the lobster may be diced or cut into escalopes – mixed with mushrooms, optional – and bound with lobster sauce (page 284, *Practical Cookery*). Pages 282–3, *Practical Cookery*, give examples of popular hot lobster dishes served in the half shell.

- Before using, what two parts of meat must be discarded after the lobster has been cut in half?

……………………………………………………………………………………………………

- When dressing a hot lobster dish in the half shell, why is it important to place a little sauce in the bottom of the shell before the meat is added?

……………………………………………………………………………………………………

Lobsters can be grilled or barbecued, in which case they may be three-quarter boiled, removed from the cooking liquor, split in half, sprinkled with melted butter and cooked for a short period of time on or under a hot grill. If the lobsters are not pre-boiled but grilled entirely from the raw state, they will tend to become tough.

- What are the two danger signs to look for before preparing and cooking lobsters?

……………………………………………………………………………………………………

- When preparing mussels for cooking, ……………………… the shells, ……………………… and drain.
- If mussels are to be cooked in a thick-bottomed pan with a tight-fitting lid as soon as they have been washed, it is not necessary to add any liquid. True or false? ………………………
- How long will mussels take to cook over a fierce heat, 1–2 min., 2–3 min., 4–5 min. or 6–7 min.?

……………………………………………………………………………………………………

- After mussels are cooked, what further inspection is required before they can be served and why?

……………………………………………………………………………………………………

- After mussels are cooked and drained, the cooking liquor should be retained as the basis for any sauce. True or false? ....
- To prepare a dish of moules marinière, which is one of the most traditional ways of serving mussels, what four ingredients are required?

....

....

- What is used to give the above sauce a light consistency?

....

Prawns, scampi, shrimp and crawfish can be cooked by shallow frying, stir-frying or deep frying. When deep fried, scampi may be passed through a light batter or flour, egg and crumbled (page 283, *Practical Cookery*).

- When deep frying bread crumbed scampi, why is it important to shake off all surplus crumbs and lightly roll the surfaces in order to firm them?

....

7   The main contamination threats when preparing and cooking fresh shellfish are:

a   The transfer of food poisoning bacteria by using the same preparation areas, equipment and utensils for preparing cooked and uncooked products.
- Give an example.

....

b   The transfer of food poisoning bacteria from unhygienic equipment, utensils and preparing methods.
- Give an example.

....

c   The transfer of food poisoning bacteria from the mouth, nose, open cuts and sores and unclean hands to food.
- Give an example.

....

d   Uncovered food contaminated by pests carrying bacteria.
- Give an example.

....

e Not disposing of waste or storing unused items in the correct manner.
- Give an example.

....

f Contamination from unclean shellfish or other matter from the sea.
- Give an example.

....

8 It is important to keep preparation and cooking areas hygienic so as to:
a Prevent contamination of food by food poisoning bacteria.
- Give an example.

....

b Prevent pest infestation and unpleasant odours from arising.
- Give an example.

....

c Ensure that standards of cleanliness are maintained.
- Give an example.

....

d Comply with the law.
- Give an example.

....

9 Time and temperature are important when cooking fresh shellfish:
a To ensure correctly cooked shellfish dishes, e.g. cooking at too high temperature for too long will ruin any shellfish.
- Give an example.

....

b To prevent food poisoning.
- Give an example.

....

c To prevent shrinkage.
- Give an example.

....

d To ensure that loss of nutritional value of prepared food is minimised.
- Give an example.

....

Record of Achievement – Completion of Unit 2ND14

Candidate's signature: _____

Assessor's signature: _____

Date: _____

Cook-chill food

Information on cook-chill will be found in *The Theory of Catering*, 8th Edition

2ND15.1 *Portion, pack and blast chill foods*

Cook-chill is a system of preparing, cooking and rapid chilling foods within a prescribed time and storing at a temperature of 0.3°C prior to regeneration immediately before serving.

Prolonged storage for up to five days (including the day of production and the final service) can be undertaken without adversely affecting the bacteriological and eating quality of the food. Prepared chilled products where re-heating is carried out should be considered cook-chill catering. It is essential that:

a Preparation areas and equipment are planned with hygiene in mind. They should be inspected by the local environmental health officer.

b Equipment is in safe working order.

c Planning makes maximum use of labour, time and materials.

d A daily schedule is compiled to assist the planning process. Daily schedules also provide management with the product processing information. Schedules identify dishes to be produced, production times, chilling times and staffing. They will also identify any delays in preparation or production.

An example of a daily schedule.

Date	Establishment
Dishes to be produced	*No. of portions*
1. Chicken chasseur	300
2. Navarin of lamb	250
3. Fillet of cod Duglére	300
4. Ratatouille pancakes	50

Blast chilling times

1. 1 hour
2. 50 minutes
3. 1½ hour
4. 55 minutes

Production

Start time
1. 9.15 am
2. 10.00 am
3. 10.30 am
4. 12.00 pm

Finish time
2.30 pm
1.15 pm
12.30 pm
2.00 pm

Staff

James Brown
Matthew Johnson
Mary Donnely
Agnes O'Reilly

- Draw up your own schedule for one dish of your own choice.

Date

Dish to be produced

....

Blast chilling time

....

Start time

....

Staff

....

Establishment

No. of portions

....

....

Finish time

....

....

1   How should preparation areas be cleaned prior to portioning and packaging chilled foods?

....

....

2 Name three problems that may occur in a cook-chill system, and who the problems should be reported to.

Problem	**Report to**
Product insufficiently cooled before packaging	Kitchen supervisor

....

....

....

Chilled food should be transported in refrigerated vans or insulated containers. All food must remain undamaged during storage to prevent transfer of bacteria.

3 State why food containers must remain undamaged during handling and transportation.

....

....

4 If four ingredients are not delivered fresh and are not of the right quality this will cause quality control problems. Why?

....

....

- Why should chilling commence within 30 minutes of the food being cooked?

....

- Why should food be chilled down to a temperature of 3°C and the storage life not to exceed five days?

....

- If the food exceeds 5°C, it must be consumed within 12 hours or discarded. Why?

....

- At a temperature of 10°C, food should be consumed
.... or ....?

5 How should temperature control be monitored?

....

• Why should it be carefully monitored?

....

• Labelling is essential to inform the end user that the product is safe and to ensure that it is refrigerated to its prime eating quality.
Complete the following label:

Name of dish   **Chicken chasseur**

No. of portions   4

Store at ....°C for max .... days

Reheat at .... for .... in a convection oven

---

Labels may also be colour coded in order to identify different dishes on certain days of the week.

• List suitable packaging containers:

....

....

....

• Dish recording is essential in order to track the process and to match the actual process to a specified process sheet. Complete the following dish recording:

Name of dish	**Chicken chasseur**
No. of portions	300
Number of chickens used	....
Storage procedures	stored at 3°C for two days
Preparation	prepared at 10°C kitchen temperature
Stored at	3°C in cold room for 24 hours
Shallow fried at	.........................°C
Simmered in sauce at	.........................°C
For	.... min.
Blast chilled at	.........................°C
For	.... min.
Portioned into	.... containers
Stored at	.................°C for .... days

- Raw materials must be of the highest quality and freshness. Why?

....

Temperature is a crucial factor at each stage of the cook-chill process; it is important that the food is received in good condition and at the right temperature.
- How should raw items be stored?

....

- Personal hygiene and food hygiene are essential. Outline six personal hygiene procedures you would recommend when working in a cook-chill environment.

....

....

....

- Name five main course dishes suitable for cook-chill.

....

....

....

- Name five desserts suitable for cook-chill.

....

....

....

(Check the above items with your tutor.)

- In order to prevent food poisoning, which special factors have to be taken into account during the cook-chill process?

....

....

....

- Give three reasons why all food containers should be sealed and labelled correctly before storage.

  ....

  ....

  ....

- Portions must be controlled when filling containers because this enables the management to control costs and it avoids waste. State two other ways in which waste can be avoided.

  ....

- Portion control maintains a consistent standard in portion size and quality, and it maintains customer expectation and satisfaction. State two other ways you would maintain customer expectation and satisfaction.

  ....

  ....

6 Most soups and sauces can now be successfully chilled, but those with a high fat or egg yolk content need a certain amount of recipe modification. Why is this?

  ....

7 Briefly explain how chilling helps prolong the storage life of cook-chill dishes.

  ....

8 The chilling process must begin as soon as possible after completion of the cooking and portioning processes.

  ....

  - The food should be chilled at 3°C (37°F) within a period of ....

9 What temperature should the food be reheated/regenerated to? ....

10 Briefly describe the main purpose of a finishing kitchen.

  ....

11 Name other types of food other than chilled food which may be prepared in a finishing kitchen to complement the menu.

....

12 The distribution method for cook-chill must ensure that the required temperature of below 3°C (37°F) is maintained throughout the period of transport. Why?

....

13 If the temperature of the food exceeds 5°C (41°F) during transportation what should happen to the food?

....

14 Briefly explain what you understand by lack of due diligence.

....

15 Why should the caterer keep documentary evidence?

....

16 To avoid the danger of cook-chill it is essential to:
a Maintain high standards of hygiene.

b ....

c ....

17 State why the employment colour coding is important in the cook-chill process.

....

18 State any items of equipment which should be colour coded.

....

<u>2ND15.2</u> *Store cook-chill food*

1 Cooked food can be kept for five days, including the days of production and consumption provided that the temperature of the cold store is maintained at between 0°C and 3°C. Should the temperature exceed 5°C, the food should be

consumed within 12 hours. Should the food exceed 10°C it must be discarded.
- For what reasons should cooked food be reheated quickly before serving?

....

....

- Food which is served cold must be consumed within ....
  hours after removal from the chilled storage.
- Food once reheated must be served .... and all unconsumed food
  should be ....
- What is meant by shelf life?

....

- Stock rotation procedures are essential in maintaining the delivery of a quality
  product. To achieve this, stock is used in order of use by date and not in excess of
  .... specifications.
- State why and how stock rotation will assist in reducing wastage.

....

....

....

- Stock rotation will also help to prevent food poisoning. Why?

....

....

- Storage areas must be secured from unauthorised access to prevent
  theft/pilferage from storage areas, and to prevent vandalism of storage areas.
  Name two other reasons.

....

....

2 Where satellite kitchens are involved, the distribution of chilled food requires precise
   organisation in order to avoid temperature fluctuation. How should temperature
   fluctuation be avoided in distribution?

....

- What type of equipment is required for regeneration?

....

- Chilled foods may support the growth of *Lysteria monocytogenes*. Why?

....

....

- *Lysteria* causes a food-borne disease which can be fatal to certain groups of people. Name these groups.

....

- Why should great care be taken when reheating chilled food by microwave?

....

....

- Name any non-microbiological changes that may occur to food.

....

....

The storage period before reheating and consumption, certain products deteriorate in quality.

3   Storage can affect the flavour of:
Certain chilled foods after three days. Name two types of food this may affect.

....

Chilled meats without sauces can develop ....
Fatty foods tend to develop off flavours due to fat ....
Vegetables may .... and develop a .... flavour.
Dishes which contain large amounts of starch may taste .... after the chilled storage time.

4   Containers must protect, and in some cases enhance, the quality of the product at all stages. It must assist in the rapid chilling, safe storage and effective reheating, therefore the container must be:

a Sturdy to withstand chilling, handling and reheating.

b ....

c ....

d ....

e ....

5 What is a cryogenic batch chiller?

....

6 State three types of reheating equipment.

....

7 Why is stock rotation especially important for cook-chill foods?

....

8 Why is it important to secure storage areas from unauthorised access?

....

9 Why is it important to keep storage areas and equipment hygienic when storing cook-chill foods?

....

10 State what you consider to be the correct clothing to be worn for the following types of people working in a cook-chill operation.
Chef: ....
Supervisor: ....
Kitchen hand: ....
Lorry driver: ....
General assistant: ....

11 Why is the wearing of correct industrial clothing important?

....

12 What do you understand by:

   a product contamination?

....

   b airborne contamination?

....

Record of Achievement – Completion of Unit 2ND15

Candidate's signature: _____

Assessor's signature: _____

Date: _____

Cook-freeze food

Information on cook-freeze will be found in *The Theory of Catering*, 8th Edition

2ND16.1 *Portion, pack and blast-freeze foods*

1 Cook-freeze production uses a system similar to cook-chill. Recipes usually have to be modified, to enable products to be freezer stable. Modified starches are used in sauces so that during reheating and regeneration the sauce does not separate.

2 The ability to freeze cooked dishes and prepared foods, as distinct from the storage of chilled foods in a refrigerator or already frozen commodities in a deep freeze, allows the caterer to make more productive use of kitchen staff. Name two other advantages that cook-freeze offers the caterer.

....

....

Foods	Dish	Modification
Poultry	Chicken sauté–chasseur	Sauces made with modified starch
Beef	....	....
Fish	....	....
Vegetables	....	....
Sauces	Mornay/red wine	Made with modified starch
Desserts	Chocolate mousse	....

3 Why do recipes often have to be modified in order to be freezer stable?

....

4   Why must freezing be carried out very rapidly?

....

- Food must be reduced to a temperature of at least ....°C within 90 minutes.
- Blast freezers are able to hold 20 to 400 kg per batch. What is this in imperial measurement?
  20 to 400 kg = ... to .... lb.
- Deep-freeze temperatures prevent the multiplication of micro-organism but do not .... them.
- Name two modified starches used in cook-freeze processes.
- The cooked food must be carefully portioned, in suitable containers. Give two examples of suitable containers.

....

- Portions must be carefully controlled when filling containers:
  To avoid ....
  To ....
  To maintain a consistent standard in the ....
  To maintain ....
- All food containers must be sealed and labelled correctly before storage to prevent contamination of food. Give four examples of how to prevent contamination of food during the cook-freeze process.

....

....

....

....

- It is essential to ensure correct storage procedures for each type of food before processing. Why is this? Give an example.

....

....

5   Blast freezing takes place at what temperature?

....

6   Special attention must be paid to quality control and hygiene. Why?

    ....

7   Why should all preparation and cooking areas be kept scrupulously clean and the
    equipment in working order?

    ....

8   The cooking process is of utmost importance and will affect the overall quality of the
    finished product.
    • In relation to the above statement, explain why time and temperature are
      important in the cooking process.

    ....

    ....

9   State why a delay in between preparation nand cooking may cause problems.

    ....

10 Why should temperature probes be used to check the centre of the food?

    ....

11 The food is divided into portions, arranged in trays and is immediately frozen.
    • A blast-freezing tunnel exposes the food to a vigorous flow of ....
      ....
      until the items are frozen solid and the temperature is reduced to at least ....
    • The reduction in temperature must take place within a period of ....
      hours.
    • Name one other type of freezing process.

    ....

12 How should re-usable containers be cleaned after use?

    ....

13 Why is it advisable for assistants involved in portioning and packaging to wear food
    handling gloves?

    ....

14 Portions should be controlled when filling the containers to:

Standardise costs.

.... costs.

....

....

Allow the sealing to be properly completed.

....

15 Food containers must be sealed correctly before storage in order to:
Prevent spoilage due to contact with cold air.

....

....

16 What legal requirements do people involved in the cook-chill process have to adhere to?

....

17 Problems which arise during the cook-chill process must be reported to the appropriate person. Why?

....

18 What type of clothing should be worn for the following people involved in the cook-chill operation?

a Kitchen supervisor: ....

b Kitchen manager: ....

c Sectional chef: ....

d Kitchen assistant: ....

e Storeperson: ....

• Why should the correct clothing be worn?

....

19 State the importance of stock rotation when operating a cook-freeze system.

....

20 Why should a cook-freeze kitchen manager keep records?
   • What type of records should be kept?

....

21 Food items during storage must remain undamaged. Why?

....

22 Why should storage areas be secured from unauthorised access?

....

23 Food should be stored in the accepted manner, on shelves and banks above the floor away from the door and with enough space around to allow the cold air to circulate. Why?

....

....

24 Freezer temperatures must be maintained during distribution. What do the Department of Health guidelines state?

....

25 Regeneration equipment must be at the correct temperature and in working order. What is the correct procedure for regeneration?

....

2ND16.2 *Store cook-freeze foods*

1 Containers must protect food against oxidation during storage and allow it to be both cooked and heated quickly. They must be watertight, non-tainting and easily disposable or re-usable. Lids must be tight fitting or be machine sealable, so that no moisture is lost and the risk of microbiological contamination is virtually eliminated.

- What is the meaning of the word oxidation?

....

- Containers come in a variety of materials. List three types of materials.

....

....

....

- Containers are available as single portion packs. Name two other sizes of container.

....

2 The main production unit and often the finishing kitchens in distribution units have deep freezers or freezer rooms where the food is stored once it has been frozen. These must be able to keep the temperature in a range from −20 to ....°C (−4 to ....°F).

   It is also very important that the equipment is powerful enough to keep the temperature at this level.

   Frozen packaged food has to be delivered to finishing kitchens at the same temperature that it left the deep freeze. Insulated containers are used for short distances, for longer distance refrigerated vans are used.
   - Refrigerated vans maintain low temperatures by the following:
     1 By a special mechanical ....
     2 By solid blocks of ....
     3 By a system of ....
     4 By a special ....

3 Name the stock rotation principles which are essential when using frozen products.

....

....

....

....

4 The finishing kitchen is where the cook-freeze product is regenerated. Explain what a thawing cabinet is.

....

....

....

5   Name the four types of equipment used to regenerate the food.

   ....

   ....

   ....

6   Labels should carry the right information about the product and this information must be easily read. The information should include the production and eat-by date, storage life, instructions for use and what two other items?

   ....

   ....

   • In labelling, what is meant by a disclaimer?

   ....

   ....

7   Why does food separate or break up after regeneration?

   ....

8   What would cause meat or fish to taste rancid?

   ....

9   Why does pastry on coated food become soggy?

   ....

10   What causes freezer burn?

   ....

Record of Achievement – Completion of Unit 2ND16

Candidate's signature: _____

Assessor's signature: _____

Date: _____

Unit 2ND17

Clean and maintain cutting equipment

Read pages 34–37 of *Practical Cookery*.

1 Before using any type of cutting equipment it is important to understand the following.
   a Equipment *must* be turned off and dismantled before and during cleaning.
   b Work should be planned and time appropriately allocated to meet daily schedules.
   c Equipment must be cleaned in accordance with laid-down procedures.
   d Correct cleaning equipment and materials must be used.
   e Cleaned equipment must be clean, dry, ready for use and must satisfy health, safety and hygiene regulations.
   f Cleaning equipment and areas must be correctly cleaned and where appropriate stored after use.
   g Appropriate action must be taken to deal with unexpected situations within an individual's responsibility.
   h All work must be carried out in an organised and efficient manner taking account of priorities and laid-down procedures.
      Mandolines can be one of the most lethal pieces of equipment in the kitchen *if* care and common sense are not used. After use, mandolines should be carefully washed in warm or hot detergent water, rinsed in clean water and carefully dried. It is wise to think of the action of the mandoline being as drastic as that of the guillotine, substituting a finger top for the head!

2 Add four pieces of equipment to the list below that are classified as dangerous under the prescribed Dangerous Machines Order 1964, and for each entry give two examples of their use:
   Worm-type mincing machine.
   Dough mixers.
   Pie and tart making machines.
   Circular knife slicing machines.

   ....

   ....

   ....

   ....

a What two documents should always be kept close to any food processing machine?

....

b Give six examples of use for the food mixer.

....

....

....

c Why should the motor of any food processing machine never be overloaded? Give one example of how this can happen.

....

d What is the tell-tale sign of an overloaded machine engine?

....

e What is the correct procedure for cleaning a machine after use?

....

f What is a vertical high-speed cuttermixer or bowl cutter? Give examples of its use.

....

....

g Food processors are versatile machines, but what is the one operation they are not suitable for? ....

3 What is the function of a liquidiser or blender? Give examples of its use.

....

....

• When liquidising hot foods, e.g. soup, what precaution must be taken and why?

....

4 Food slicers can be lethal if used by a careless worker. What are the five safety rules that must be followed when using a food slicer?

   1 Ensure that no material likely to damage the blades, e.g. bone, is included in the food to be sliced. Otherwise the result will be to ....

   2 ....

   3 ....

   4 ....

   5 Extra care must be taken when the blades are exposed.

5 Hand-operated and electric chipping machines are available. What is the correct way to use and maintain a chipping machine?

....

6 Why should a food masher be washed, rinsed and dried immediately after use?

....

7 As a general rule, after switching off the electricity all food processing machines should be dismantled after use, thoroughly washed, dried and re-assembled for the next use.

   • The reasons why equipment is turned off and dismantled before cleaning are to prevent accidents and injury, to ensure thorough cleaning, and to comply with the law.

8 State how the following pieces of equipment should be dismantled and cleaned:

   a gravity feed slicing machine ....

   b food processor ....

   c mincing machine ....

9   Sketch a rotary knife chopping machine bowl chopper.

- List four problems associated with cleaning large mechanical equipment.

....

....

....

....

10   What training should staff be given in order to safely clean equipment?

....

....

11   Cutting equipment should be turned off and dismantled before cleaning. Why?

....

12   What are the main dangers that the kitchen employee has to be aware of?

....

13   What precautions should the kitchen employee take when dismantling cutting equipment?

....

....

14   How should portable cutting equipment be stored?

....

15   Compile a cleaning schedule for a piece of cutting equipment for which you are familiar.

....

....

....

....

....

....

....

....

....

....

....

16   What piece of legislation governs health and safety practices?

....

17   The manufacturer's instructions and recommendations are important for maintaining and storing cutting equipment.
Comment on how cutting equipment is stored in the kitchen that you are familiar with.

....

....

....

....

18 Complete the following:
Cutting equipment must be kept clean and in ....
Faulty equipment must be clearly labelled, isolated to prevent use and reported
to ....
Cutting equipment must be handled safely and lifted using ....
....

19 How should the storage equipment area be kept?

....

....

20 List the advantages of a maintenance contract.

....

....

....

21 Regular inspection should be made of all cutting equipment in the kitchen. Why?

....

22 Using diagrams, show how heavy or bulky equipment should be safely lifted.

23 Storage areas must be kept secured from unauthorised access. Why?

....

Record of Achievement – Completion of Unit 2ND17

Candidate's signature: _____

Assessor's signature: _____

Date: _____

Unit 2ND20

Prepare and cook battered fish and chipped potatoes

2ND20.1 *Prepare batter for frying*

Read pages 261–264 of *Practical Cookery*.

1 Why is personal hygiene important to observe when preparing frying batters?

....

2 How should preparation equipment be cleaned prior to commencing work?

....

  • How should preparation areas be cleaned prior to commencing work?

....

3 List the ingredients required to produce 400 g (1 lb) of yeast batter.
    400 g (1 lb) of strong flour.

....

....

....

....

4 List two alternative batters to yeast.

....

....

5 If the ingredients required for the recipe are not of the correct standard or type, when and to whom should you report?

....

6 How should batter which is not required for immediate use be stored?

....

7 What equipment would you use in your establishment if you had to prepare frying batter for 250 portions of fried fish?

....

• How would this equipment be cleaned?

....

8 How long should frying batter be allowed to relax before use?

....

9 What is the shelf life of a refrigerated frying batter?

....

10 Compare the differences in producing a batter by hand and using a machine.

....

11 Briefly describe an automatic batter mixer.

....

....

12 What measuring equipment do you need in order to produce 100 portions of batter?

....

13 How much batter do you require for the following:
250 × 100 g (4 oz) portions of cod: ....
300 × 75 g (3 oz) fillets of plaice: ....
500 × 100 g (4 oz) portions of haddock: ....

14 Describe the overall appearance of a freshly made frying batter.

....

....

15 When using mechanical equipment to prepare large quantities of frying batter, what health and safety rules must you follow?

....

....

16 Give an example of a safe working practice when producing a frying batter manually.

....

17 A frying batter could be contaminated after prolonged storage in a refrigerator. How could contamination take place?

....

18 Is time and temperature important when preparing frying batter?

....

19 What is a safe storing temperature?

....

20 The colour of the frying batter is an important quality point, the consistency is another. Name one other quality point that should be taken into account when preparing batter.

....

21 Why is it important to test the consistency of the batter before frying takes place?

....

22 If the consistency is inadequate what ingredient could be added to improve its frying importance?

....

23 Why should the batter rest before frying?

....

24 The purpose of the batter is to protect the food from:

Overcooking
Flavour impairment
....
....
....

25 State the main advantages of using a convenience batter mix.

....

2ND20.2 *Prepare and cook battered fish*

1 The quality points for fresh fish are:
The eyes of the fish are full and not sunken.
The gills are bright red in colour and not ....

....

....

....

2 What weight should a portion of fish be as a general guide:
a Off the bone? ....
b On the bone? ....

3 Briefly describe the filleting of:
a flat fish ....
b round fish ....

4 How does the skinning of Dover sole differ from the skinning of other flat fish?

....

....

5 Describe the following preparation for fish:
Goujons: ....
Goujonettes: ....
Supreme: ....

6 If the fish has an unpleasant smell, what should you do?

....

7 Before frying, the portions of fish should be coated in flour prior to being dipped in the frying batter. Why?

....

8 Frying oils often contain an anti-spattering agent. What does this mean?

....

9 What makes vegetable oil a suitable frying medium?

....

10 How should the battered fish be placed in the hot oil?

....

11 What is the suitable frying temperature for cooking fillets of battered cod?

....

12 State four safety factors which have to be considered when frying fish.

....

....

....

....

13 List the small equipment required for deep frying fish:
Spider

....

....

....

....

14 After the frying is completed what procedure should be followed to ensure health and safety?

....

15 At what temperature should freshly fried fish be stored?

....

16 State how frozen portion fillets of fish should be prepared and cooked.

....

17 Raw fish may be a potential contamination threat, how should raw fish be treated in order to prevent any possible contamination from spreading?

....

18 The overall quality of cooked battered fish may be judged by:
a The crispness of the batter.
b The colour of the batter.

c ....

d ....

19 Explain the following terms:
Frying temperature: ....

Smoking point: ....

Flash point: ....

20 Time and temperature are important factors during each stage of the preparation and cooking process. Explain why.

....

21   Sketch a cool zone fryer, labelling and describing what is meant by the cool zone.

22   Why is it important to take care of the cooking oil?

....

23   Why should the cooking oil be covered when not in use?

....

24   What do you understand by the term 'recovery time'?

....

25   If the battered fish is placed in cooking oil which is at too lower a temperature, what effect does this have on the product?

....

   • If the temperature is too high what effect does this have on the product?

....

26   What do you understand by carbonisation?

....

27   What is the purpose of filtering the cooking oil?

....

28   Which cooking oils are more suitable for people who are concerned with healthy eating?

....

29   How can over absorption of cooking oil be avoided?

....

2ND20.3   *Prepare and cook chipped potatoes*

Read pages 571–572 of *Practical Cookery*.

1   State the hygienic practices that should be observed when preparing chipped potatoes.

....

2   Name four potato varieties which are most suitable for chipped potatoes.

....

....

3   If the potatoes are not of the right quality, who should be informed?

....

4   List examples of different shapes for deep fried potatoes.

....

5   Briefly describe an automatic chipping machine.

....

....

6   At what temperature should chipped potatoes be blanched?

....

  • At what temperature for finishing?

....

7   The quality of chipped potatoes relies on the blanching and finishing process to produce the texture and crispness. Describe the correct colour.

....

8   Describe how the preparation, cooking areas and equipment should be cleaned after use.

....

....

9   List the items of small equipment you require for preparing, cooking and serving deep fried potatoes.

....

....

....

10 State any problems that may be associated with:
Large equipment: ....
Freshness of potatoes: ....

11 List the advantages of using pre-prepared chipped potatoes.
  a Labour saving.

  b ....

c ....

d ....

12 How should frozen chipped potatoes be cooked and served?

....

13 List six safety points which must be observed when preparing, cooking and serving chipped potatoes.

....

....

....

14 Why is frying chips at the correct temperature so important?

....

15 Why is it important to lift heavy or bulk items using approved safe methods?

....

16 What are the main contamination threats when storing raw and cooked chipped potatoes?

....

17 The frying medium must be filtered and changed at regular intervals. Why?

....

18 At what temperature should cooked chipped potatoes be stored?

....

19 For how long should cooked chipped potatoes be stored at the correct temperature?

....

20 Does reducing the amount of salt added to chipped potatoes contribute to healthy catering practices?

....

Record of Achievement – Completion of Unit 2ND20

Candidate's signature: _____

Assessor's signature: _____

Date: _____

Unit 2ND21

Prepare, assemble and cook pizza products

2ND21.1 *Prepare pizza products ready for cooking*

Read pages 737–738 of *Practical Cookery*.

1 State how preparation areas and suitable equipment should be cleaned ready for use.

....

....

2 List the ingredients required to produce a pizza base.

....

....

....

3 Name six more suitable toppings for pizza which you are familiar with.
Tomato, ham, pepper and mozzarella cheese

....

....

....

....

....

4 Any problems associated with ingredients should be reported to whom?

....

5 State the basic preparation methods for a pizza dough.

....

6 List the equipment that you would require to prepare basic pizza dough.

....

7 At what temperature should you store ingredient toppings if they are not required for immediate use?

....

8 State what the following equipment would be used for when producing pizzas:
Prover: ....
Retarder: ....
Food mixer: ....
Slicing/cutting machine: ....
Chilled preparation: ....
Table: ....
Refrigerator: ....
Freezer: ....
Containers: ....

9 List four fresh vegetables which could be used for producing pizza.

....

....

10 List four pre-prepared or convenience foods which may be used in pizza toppings.

....

....

11 Why should pizza dough be proved?

....

12 List the ingredients and quantity for 20 portions of vegetarian pizza.

....

....

....

....

....

....

....

....

13 Name five hygiene practices that should be observed when producing pizza.

....

....

....

....

....

14 In assessing the quality of pizza explain the following:
Texture: ....
Flavour: ....
Aroma: pleasant, pungent smell
Appearance: regular shape, colourful
Consistency: ....

15 State why time and temperature is important when preparing pizza products.

....

16 Give a four portion recipe for a pizza which could be classified as a healthy product.

....

....

....

....

....

....

....

....

2ND21.2 *Assemble and cook pizza product*

1 Describe how a pizza base should be assembled.

....

....

2 How should a pizza be packed for a 'take away' service?

....

3 At what temperature should pizzas be baked?

....

4 Apart from yeast dough which other types of base could be used for pizza toppings?

....

5 Name three different herbs which are used on pizza.

....

6 There are a number of different convenience sauces and toppings on the market. Name different varieties.

....

7 What health and safety precautions do you need to consider when baking, cutting and serving pizza?

....

8 State the safe hot temperature for storing freshly baked pizzas.

....

9 How should the preparation and baking area be cleaned after production?

....

Record of Achievement – Completion of Unit 2ND21

Candidate's signature: _____

Assessor's signature: _____

Date: _____